THE WITHERING PROMISE

THE WITHERING PROMISE

Memoirs from the Heart of a Failing Health System

DOUGLAS ONYANCHA NGOGE

EXCELLER BOOKS®
A GLOBAL PRESS

The Withering Promise
Memoirs from the Heart of a Failing Health System

Cover by Exceller Books

Print ISBN: 978-93-47397-96-7

Published in India in 2026 by Exceller Books,
An imprint of GE Group,
G1, Dream Apartment, Degree College Road, Belgharia,
Kolkata, 700056, India
www.excellerbooks.com

EXCELLER BOOKS®
A GLOBAL PRESS

Author's Note

Do not live your life with anger and hate in your heart. You'll only be hurting yourself more than the people you hate. It is very important to generate a good attitude, a good heart, as much as possible. From this, happiness in both the short term and the long term for both yourself and others will come.

Acknowledgements

This work would not have been possible without the support of my family. No one has been more important to me in the pursuit of this work than my wife and family members.

I would like to thank my parents, whose love and guidance are with me in whatever I pursue. They are the ultimate role models.

Most importantly, I would like to thank my loving and supportive wife, Lilian Bwari, who provides me with unending inspiration.

I am grateful to all of those with whom I have had the pleasure to work during this time.

Introduction

The book discusses the writer's experiences. It begins with motivation, encouragement, and inspiration; the writer is encouraging the reader to keep trying and remain dedicated to their dreams. The writer gives his own encounter with poverty. He continues to talk about work experience and inhuman activities happening in hospitals, how the patients are exploited. The work addresses the political elite. Gives a story of the current government's letdowns. In the book, the story of the country's education and health systems is presented, along with the challenges resulting from the COVID-19 pandemic.

He talks about the parenting style. Gives a story of his family at the end of the book. All the illustrations, examples, and stories provided explain how people are ravaged by poverty, and at every level of service delivery, corruption inevitably arises.

Table of Contents

Chapter 1

I do not know what you are expecting from this book. We do not share the same experiences or struggles, but I believe that, if you read it, we can, together, change our society, culture, beliefs, motives, attitudes, and the nation as a whole, regardless of your prior experiences.

Change occurs when each of us makes an effort towards it, but what specific change do we need? Who will bring this change? It is not something we can buy; it demands thought, effort, and sacrifice, and most importantly, not putting ourselves in the first place. But how many are willing to commit themselves to this demanding task?

For a moment, I want you to think about your past. Is it something you admire? Do you wish you could relive a moment from your earlier life—the way things were, the people, the experiences, everything that comes to mind?

What rises in your thoughts when you look back? I am sorry for those who feel tears welling up at the mere mention of "your past"—perhaps because it was painful, undesirable, or difficult. But the truth is, you cannot change your past. What you can shape is your future.

The good news—and what truly matters—is that you are here, in this moment, and you do not have to be weighed down by your past unless you choose to be.

I often hear people say, "I miss my childhood days and experiences." But how many truly reflect on it? How many have tried to express what they feel, and to whom, and how, and why? And then what happens?

And then someone comes forward to tell their story.

This is my story.

But what relevance does it hold for you, and for the society we live in?

The boy finds himself in a family of eleven siblings, not to mention the extended family, friends, and relatives who constantly come and go in their home.

Home was home not just for them, but for everyone in the village—and even for people from far beyond. And it still is, to this day. Yet, despite this, life was unfair. Their parents were unemployed, surviving as subsistence farmers. But how could they farm when there was no proper land? With the weight of life pressing in from every side, the family became the laughing stock of the village and the wider community.

People mocked them. They would say things like, "Make a football team with no food, school, and clothes privileges!" Little did they know, God watches from above.

One day, his sister was walking along the school compound with her friends and cousins. One of them suddenly pointed and said:

"Your dad!"

"My dad?" she asked.

"Yes!

Where is he?"

"See, he's coming over there."

"But how did you recognise him?"

"Hey, who doesn't know his only black suit after all these years!?"

From that moment, she fell silent for the rest of the journey. Those were just her friends, but she remembers that moment vividly to this day.

It may not strike you at first, and it may not trigger anything immediately, but please keep reading.

Call them what you will, but to him, they were uncles. Every cruel scene they created in their home, he remembers to this day—including the plot to kill his mother during a planned visit to a friend, and schemes to make sure we never finished school. I recall one Sunday after church, a cousin tried to poison the entire family by slipping poison into the drinking water pot, only to be caught red-handed by my mother.

They all went to school. But how? Who would have thought anything good could come out of that family? To the haters, we were destined to perish, not to prosper.

When his mother walked through the village, women selling cereals would hide until she had passed. The reason? Your guess is as good as mine; lest she come to borrow from them again.

School was no easier. The intimidation was relentless; walking barefoot, wearing torn uniforms, going without meals, but think of his focus, his concentration in class.

One day, a friend accompanied him to the school toilet. The friend came out quickly, but he, weakened from poor meals and a meagre diet, stayed a little longer. And to make matters worse, the school toilets had no doors. Standing outside, the friend began to mock him: "Look, it's stuck! It won't move!" The embarrassment was overwhelming—but all I could do was take it as a joke.

He had to be pulled out of class to fetch vegetables for the teacher's lunch because even the teachers knew that the money from selling those vegetables might be the only income the family would see that day. Do not ask about the rest of the days—only God knows.

Home was meant to be a place of safety, a place to breathe. But there, worries never left. Under the trees, they would try to relax, playing cards and draughts. Friends, cousins, and relatives would come and stay—some only to see whether there would be anything to eat that day, to carry back stories and rumours to the village; others to consume whatever little there was, leaving the family to face emptiness the next day. By evening, misery remained. All eyes were on the gate, watching the pathway from the main road to the nearby primary school, hoping to see their mother carrying something—anything—to ease the day. It became routine, a way of life.

If you had seen them in the garden, oh my God! The type of jembes they wore, the expression on their faces…pure misery.

Days passed, but life never got easier. It was harder than most could imagine.

He watched his brothers and sisters struggle in school, each carrying their own burden, each with their own story—at home, in school, in the village, with friends.

He remembered his brother telling how he had to convince their parents that the third-born, who was in school, was sick, just to get a little extra money. The single shilling already given as pocket money was not enough to buy even Panadol for him on the way to school, kilometres away, trekking uphill over rough, dusty roads, carrying his school bag. With some pleading, they were given two extra shillings—three in total for two children in boarding school, one of them sick. How they managed to make those three shillings last the whole term...he could never understand; he was a stranger in the world of finance.

He also remembered the last day of his KCPE exam. Usually, there is joy, photos with classmates, and a celebration of finishing class eight. A friend saw him taking a photo barefoot with the headmaster and offered his own shoes to wear just for the picture, to return afterwards. They were far too big for his tiny feet. By then, he was a small boy in every sense, and the shoes—like so much in his life—didn't quite fit.

Chapter 2

In high school, life was just amazing. I progressed from first to fourth standard, though not without struggles. Being in school on and off due to fees was a challenge. My school fees were paid in an unusual way: by supplying Sukuma wiki to the school. I had to wake up very early every morning to carry it, so that no one would see me hauling a sack from home to school daily. Despite 9my efforts, I didn't achieve the grades I had hoped for.

I stayed home for a while, then worked at a nearby private academy as a teacher. Later, I was employed as a security guard with Brinks Security in Kisumu for three months. I was deployed to very insecure areas, often alone at night—foreign places, at a tender age, with no experience, not even a torch or weapon, only a whistle. I endured the cold, mosquito bites, rain, harsh environments, and mistreatment from senior staff. Meals were scarce, and I was forced to work at an industrial area during the day, then resume night duty just to survive. If I got some money for my work only one day a week, that felt like a lucky week, because the company often didn't even pay me.

One day, while working at an Indian company called United Millers, I was caught on CCTV eating mandazi flour mix. I was hungry, had no money, and no choice. The boss called me, asked for my name and ID card, insulted me, and called me an idiot. I was worried about being dismissed, looking pathetic—but to me, it was fair. At least I had something to eat that day.

I had been lured from the academy that paid me two thousand shillings per month, with promises from the security company of eighteen thousand. It sounded like a good deal, though in reality I only received three thousand eight hundred shillings. Three thousand went to house rent, and the rest had to cover the upkeep of the month for me and my brother in college.

Life was hard and only seemed to get worse. I decided to go back to school, joining form class three, this time with a clear focus on achieving my childhood dreams.

In those two years in Kisumu, I discovered my potential. I realized I had something that could define me: I was a champion in Mathematics. Perhaps it ran in my genes. My father had been recognized by his peers as a mathematics champion. He never passed the seventh grade, but maybe, had he done so, he could have become a teacher and faced none of these struggles.

I consistently earned A's in classwork and tests. I won awards in regional competitions. My only real competitor in mathematics was Simenya. Occasionally, I was given the chance to teach my classmates, although there was one unit I struggled with: a four-mark question using a log table. Still, I performed well in almost everything else, including all ten-mark questions.

I eventually earned a grade that landed me in medical school. It was a dream-come-true moment for me.

All in all, it was by God's grace.

Chapter 3

In college, coming from the background I came from, many of my fellow students thought I was from a well-off family—simply because, by God's grace, I could afford breakfast, sometimes lunch, and supper, which I often shared with my college girlfriend, who is now my beautiful and loving wife.

There were times when a friend would ask to borrow money, and I would give them even what I had saved for supper, becauseL I knew too well what it meant to go hungry. That made others think I always had enough, but the truth was different.

I kept pushing forward, and today, here I am—sitting in my office as a CEO and consultant surgeon in my own hospital, an employer of several people. God has been good. My dreams are big, and my hopes are high.

But Mr Politician, do you really know my expectations? When I stand in your rallies and you address us as "fellow Kenyans," when you come to funerals and speak, do you really understand who I am? You know I am poor. What do you expect from me? All I ask for is just a fraction of what you spend to start your car—enough to pay my bills and keep going.

And Doctor, when I stand next to you, presenting a case, do you know what my heart is truly praying for? My expectations are filled with dreams. But do dreams really come true?

These questions bombard my mind whenever I find myself in desperate situations.

That is why I appeal to everyone who has a role in shaping the well-being of students and learners: consider them fully and sincerely. Do not make someone feel as if they are begging for your help.

There is so much misery and suffering hidden within the so-called education systems. That is why some students cannot endure the journey, and many drop out.

Chapter 4

You do not own the whole world. If you keep holding on to yesterday, you will never see tomorrow. You must move forward because you are not the custodian of everything.

Sometimes, when life gets tough, I remind myself of this. And I want you to remind yourself, too. Connect the dots in your own life—do something, rise up, and act. Do not waste time arguing, just do it.

'Out there' means a lot to me. It is a place of endless possibilities. And you must be prepared for it. Step out and conquer it. Let the world know you exist. Claim your place out there. Be bold, be relentless—there is no room for laziness. Only the strong survive. Never let yourself down.

I want to learn. I want to work hard. I want to earn my share of life's rewards. And yet sometimes, I wonder why I do not enjoy the same fruits as others. That's when my instinct speaks to me. I listen to my inner self. I speak to myself. I have ambitions—great ambitions. I keep moving, keep trying, stay focused. I go for it. I believe in myself. I remind myself that I can get to where I want to be.

This dialogue is always in my mind. Can you join me in this dialogue? I believe you have one too. Listen to it. Your inner voice will change, it will grow, and it will guide you with new ideas. It never stops talking. And it keeps reminding you of the greatness you can become.

I once read that if you spend time with four millionaires, you'll probably become the fifth. But if you spend time with four fools, you'll likely become even more foolish than them. The people around you shape who you are. Surround yourself with the right ones.

Your environment is everything.

Network with the right people, because your network is your net worth.

When in the presence of greatness, stay quiet and observe. Take what you see, apply it to your own life, and use it to succeed. Seek knowledge. And remember this truth: the higher you want to go, the deeper you must go in God.

Build daily habits that lead to success.

Wake up early. Exercise. Complete your most important task. Take time to recharge. Plan your day the night before. Set clear priorities. Network with your team. Make time for your family. And do not stop when you are tired—stop only when you are done.

I am told these are the daily habits of successful people. Do you want to be one?

Happiness and satisfaction are deeply personal. I used to think the worst thing in life was ending up alone. It's not. The worst is being surrounded by people who make you feel alone.

So live your life. Take chances. Be bold. Do not wait. Because right now, you are the oldest you've ever been and the youngest you'll ever be again.

Create a life that feels good on the inside, not one that only looks good on the outside. I have learnt that life's tragedy is that we grow old too soon and wise too late. But remember: when you begin to see people's hearts instead of just their faces, life becomes clearer.

Life is too short to worry about what others think of you. Enjoy it. Have fun. Give them something worth talking about.

The hardest lessons in life often come at the worst times and through the toughest mistakes. But do not fear mistakes—they are blessings in disguise. Every setback is a setup for growth. Hold your head high and keep moving forward, no matter how much it hurts.

Sometimes the hardest lessons are the ones your soul needs most. Your past is not a mistake if you've learned from it. Gather all your experiences, all your scars, and place them in a box labelled "thank you."

Life will disappoint you. It will test you. But it cannot defeat you. Nothing is more powerful than a made-up mind.

Surround yourself with people who remind you of your worth and support your journey. Never let circumstances define you. Define yourself.

Do not give up. Do not cave in. Do not stop believing. It is not over until you win.

We are not given a good life or a bad life—we are given life. It's up to us to make it good or bad. Looking back, I realise that every rejection was not the end, but a redirection to something better.

So cherish the little things. One day, you will look back and see they were the big things.

Do not wake up with regrets. Wake up believing your day will be successful. Love those who treat you right. Let go of those who do not. Believe everything happens for a reason.

If you get a chance, take it. If it changes your life, embrace it. Never let your past imprison you—it was a lesson, not a life sentence.

Sometimes life asks you to risk everything for a dream that only you can see. If you abandon that dream, you'll realise that as you grow older, you become quieter. Life humbles you. You see how much time was wasted on nonsense.

If you do not make time to create the life you want, you will be forced to live a life you do not want.

It takes deep self-love, dedication, and determination to live your greatest life. So look within yourself. Examine every area of your life and ask:

Am I on the right path?
Am I growing mentally?
Am I growing emotionally?
Am I growing spiritually?
Am I growing economically?
Am I growing socially?

Am I growing academically?

If anything is blocking that growth—anything that keeps you from living your greatest life—have the courage to let it go.

One day, you will wake up and there will be no more time to do the things you always wanted to do. Do them now.

Life is full of irony. I often discover the value of happiness through moments of sadness. Noise teaches me the beauty of silence. Absence makes me cherish presence.

As a doctor, let me advise you: remove anger, regret, worry, resentment, guilt, and blame from your mind. You will see both your life and your health improve. Do not cry over the past—it's gone. Do not stress about the future—it hasn't arrived. Live in the present, and make it beautiful.

The greatest challenge in life is to discover who you are. Once you do, the next great challenge is to be happy with what you find.

As I grow older, I've realised that true happiness does not lie in how much money I make, how many degrees I hold, how big my house is, or how fancy my car may be. True happiness is peace, joy, and calmness in the heart and mind. What matters most to me is my family. What matters most is love. So I will love my family deeply and give love to those who truly matter. I hope you will do the same.

Today, I am more committed than ever to reuniting my family.

Mental disorders are real. Today I spoke with Dr. Mabongo, a consultant psychiatrist and medical superintendent at Mathare, the leading referral psychiatric hospital. He referred me to my local psychiatrist, Dr. Mawazo, to help address my family's struggles. Remember this: haters will rejoice when your family falls apart. Love your family. Stand by them. Help those who need your help.

A meaningful life is not about being rich, popular, highly educated, or perfect. It is about being real, being humble, and being willing to share yourself in a way that touches the lives of others.

Chapter 5

I am sharing my thoughts with you because I do not want us to go through misery just to understand how tough life can be. You do not need to go without meals or walk unclothed to know that poverty exists among us.

If my words encourage you, I just want to remind you not to let regret hold you back. Do not feel sorry for yourself. Stay focused. It's not too late. Start from where you are and keep moving forward.

Do not shrink your dreams to fit your reality. Strengthen your conviction to rise to your destiny.

Do not wait for life to get easier or better. Life will always have its challenges, so choose happiness now, or you might miss your chance.

If we all live meaningful lives based on love, we'll see that what matters isn't what we buy, but what we build. It's not about what we get, but what we give; not just our skills, but our character; not just our success, but the positive impact we leave on others and our community.

The best day of your life is when you decide to take full ownership of it. Do not make excuses or blame others. Treat your life as a gift and a journey that only you can shape. That's when your real life starts.

Happiness comes from accepting where you are and making the most of every single day. There comes a time when you must walk away from the drama and the people who create it. Surround yourself with those who make you laugh, help you forget the bad, and focus on the good. Love those who treat you right, and pray for those who do not. Just be happy.

Falling down is part of life; getting back up is what makes life worth living.

Remember, you are never too old to set another goal or dream a new dream.

Treasure life as it happens. Moments pass quickly, and one day you'll wish you had cherished them more.

The secret to success lies in your daily routine. Change what you do each day, and you will change your life. Life will only shift when you become more committed to your dreams than to your comfort zone.

Remind yourself often: the more you live in the past, the less of the future you have to enjoy.

Life is like a house party. Many people will come. Some leave early, some stay all night, some laugh with you, some laugh at you, and some arrive late. But in the end, after the fun, only a few will stay to help you clean up the mess. Most of the time, they aren't the ones who made it. These are your true friends. They are the ones who matter, so identify them and hold them close.

Know your place in people's lives and act accordingly. This isn't pride; it's self-respect. As the saying goes, there are two things you should never fight for in life: love and true friendship. They come naturally.

When problems pour into your life like unending rain, remember that God will always be your umbrella. Amen.

Consider this: a razor blade is sharp but can't cut a tree, and an axe is strong but can't cut hair. We all have our own unique purpose, so never look down on anyone.

If that still seems unclear, think about how a caterpillar becomes a butterfly—full of life and free to go anywhere.

Let each day bring you closer to your dreams. Dream to break the chains of poverty in your family's lineage.

Giving up on your dreams is as painful as losing someone you once thought you'd spend your life with. It's truly heartbreaking.

Sometimes you feel unsatisfied with your life, while someone else is dreaming of living it. For example, a child on a farm looks up at a plane and dreams of flying, while a pilot on that plane looks down at the farmhouse and dreams of coming home.

That is life. Appreciate yours and live it to the fullest.

Let's think about this: if money brought happiness, rich people would dance in the streets, but it's often poor children who dance without worry. If power meant safety, politicians and celebrities wouldn't need protection, yet they often can't sleep peacefully. People who live simply, though, sleep well and feel free.

Money is not everything.

If money could buy you a life, rich people who rush to hospitals in helicopters would be guaranteed to live. But they are not; they can still die. And these same people, many of them lawmakers, never cared to build proper health facilities for the poor, who may never even see a helicopter.

Give us a break.

And think again: if beauty and fame brought perfect relationships, then celebrities would have the happiest marriages. Yet we see breakups and betrayals everywhere.

So live simply, walk humbly, love sincerely, and do good to everyone, because in the end, you get back what you give.

You will be deeply disappointed if you expect people to treat you as you treat them. Not everyone has your heart. Be a good person in everything you do, so that when you are gone, your goodness will still be felt in the lives you touched. Give even if you have little. Smile when you can. Work when you can. Pray for others. Love without limits. Lift people up instead of pulling them down. Do all the good you can while you are alive, for wealth fades, but goodness lasts forever.

In many African cultures, children are often named after notable individuals. That is why some names disappear completely after death, while others remain alive for generations. Good people leave behind a good name. Bad people take theirs with them.

There's a saying: sugar and salt can be mixed, but ants only take the sugar. As people, we should choose what's right and avoid what doesn't fit. If you do not reach your dreams, change your approach, not your faith. Remember, trees change their leaves, not their roots. Speak kindly, have good character, and stay observant—there's so much to learn and do not waste time responding to every distraction, or you'll never reach your goals.

On your ladder to success, haters will see you walking on water and say it's because you can't swim. Do not mind them, keep moving, remain focused, go for what you want, do not let it go, because even if you dance on water, your enemies will accuse you of raising dust.

Make it your ambition to live a quiet life, to mind your own business. And mind you forget, do not ever wrestle with a pig, you'll both get dirty, but the pig will enjoy it.

Make it a habit to care for others. Remember, the job you find tough is someone else's dream, your small home is a wish for someone without shelter, and your smile is what someone struggling hopes for. Appreciate what you have and be thankful in every situation.

If you feel frustrated with your child, remember that many people who cannot have children would love to be in your place.

Try not to complain about having little money. For someone in debt, even a small amount would be a blessing.

As I've said before, always thank God no matter what your situation is.

Do good for others, even if you get nothing back. What matters most is not what you have, but how you help others grow. Keep encouraging people and helping them succeed. They will remember how you made them feel.

I spoke with my old high school English teacher and told him I'm writing a book. I promised to share a copy with him when it's finished. He congratulated me, which made me feel good. I also thought about asking him for advice on publishing.

I am told to keep going and not to worry about my speed, given that I am making progress, even if it doesn't seem like it; forward is forward, no matter how slow.

Someone once said, "Never regret any day in your life." Good days bring happiness, bad days teach you, the worst days give lessons, and the best days leave memories. Which kind of day do you want? Be ready for whatever comes.

As you go through life, avoid arguing with people who just want to bring you down. They will pull you to their level and win with experience. Choose your company wisely.

For the Bible says in Isiah 3:10: "Tell the righteous it will be well with them, for they will enjoy the fruits of their deeds."

We also find in Psalms 84:11 that the Lord bestows favour and honour; no good thing does He withhold from those who walk uprightly.

In John 16:3-8, we also find that we are told, 'I have said this to you so that in me you may have peace.' In the world, you face persecution. But take courage, I have conquered the world.

Pray to see the good in others, to forgive those who hurt you, to let go of past wrongs, and to keep your faith in God strong.

Chapter 6

As a doctor, I've learned so much from many people in all kinds of situations. Some days were easy, others were hard. It wasn't always simple, but each step brought me closer to my dreams.

That's incredible.

From my days on campus, facing tough lecturers, to my internship where I dealt with difficult senior staff, I've met so many people and seen patients with all kinds of conditions—some for the first time. I've been through a lot, but I'm still here.

I've learned that each new day feels like being born again. When I see a patient lying helpless in bed, I realise how valuable good health is. Helping someone breathe with oxygen reminds me how precious it is to breathe easily. Feeding a patient through a tube shows me how important it is to eat on your own. Assisting someone to the bathroom makes me appreciate being able to go by myself. Easing a patient's pain reminds me how fortunate it is to live without pain. Watching patients struggle in their final days teaches me the importance of doing good and making the most of life while we can.

Take a moment to think about someone who is very sick in a hospital and can't do what you are doing right now. Remember to be grateful every day.

There is agony in the hospitals.

If the walls of a hospital could talk, they would have many lessons to share. They might even remind us not to make poor choices in life.

Value your life when you have it.

Every day brings something new, and each moment is special. Waking up with a clear mind is a gift I don't take for granted. I've learned to be grateful and to change how I think. When I see patients who have lost their memories because of illness, I realise how important it is to wake up each day with a healthy mind and good memories.

I once thought my own struggles were difficult, but I've come to see that real struggle is wondering when you'll get out of a hospital bed, speak again, see again, walk, or feed yourself.

I hear these questions from patients every day, often through tears and pain. I have my own struggles, too. This work has never been easy for me, but I see it as my calling.

I struggle. I struggle.

Some struggles are as basic as wondering how to feed your children today or whether you can afford a loaf of bread.

Or, I am terminally ill, how long have I got left to live?

My struggles…

Sometimes, I find myself asking how I can get more of what I already have.

Realising all of this has changed me deeply.

I appreciate all that I have and enjoy what I own.

And I stopped worrying about the things I do not own today.

Peter spent the whole night fishing in the same river but caught nothing. Yet, in the morning, that same river gave him an abundance of fish. The difference was when Jesus asked if he had caught anything, and Peter said no, Jesus did not tell him to find another river. Instead, He told him to cast his net deeper.

In the same way, when life feels like it is going in the wrong direction, the answer is not always to change your job, your church, your spouse, or to give up. The answer is to deepen your faith. Trust God more. Draw closer to Jesus. Believe that He will provide, heal, restore, uplift, deliver, revive, and bless you with His favour. May the Lord give you the grace to go deeper in faith.

Amen.

Chapter 7

When I was growing up, I believed everyone close to me was a true friend. I didn't realise how much life can change over time.

I knew that a poor person has no friends.

Experiencing poverty often drives your friends away.

The lives of the rich and the poor are worlds apart.

When you try to talk to people from wealthy families, they sometimes look at you with suspicion, as if you are a threat. They wonder, 'What could this nobody possibly have to say to us?'

People do not like good thoughts; they like good looks.

If you don't look like them, they won't let you join their group. Be careful who you trust, because some people will mock you, try to bring you down, and discourage your dreams. They might say things like, 'Don't tell us about your future plans. What does your family have that will help you succeed? You'll never be more than a beggar. You don't belong with us.'

It is traumatising to remember such sentiments.

Now, the same people who once said those things watch as I drive by and wave from my car. I see them standing by the road, tired, wearing dirty clothes, some barefoot and in torn trousers. I leave them talking, surprised at how things have changed. Life can turn around; the same God who gives some people a seat can have others sitting on the ground.

Now, even those who once doubted or criticised are facing their own struggles.

These days, I've realized that people respect money more than the person. When someone gets money, it changes everything about them—their lifestyle, thoughts, class, and even their character.

The people you respect, trust, and even love the most can end up hurting you the most—especially if you ever dare to ask them for money.

The truth is, sometimes when someone from a humble background gets a little money, they may behave even worse than those who come from wealthy families. It sounds simple, but when you try to explain it, people often hesitate to say it out loud, and that's what makes it complicated.

I've learned that when you're happy, you just enjoy the music, but when you're sad, you really understand the words.

I've also realised that two things can define you: your patience when you have nothing, and your attitude when you have everything.

Here's a bit of advice: don't rely too much on anyone, not even family. Even your own shadow disappears when it's dark.

Let's all have good intentions and wish the best for others.

Think of others this way: one day, your friend, sibling, neighbour, or partner will achieve their dreams, and you'll be there to support them every step of the way.

It won't cost you anything to wish someone well. If you can, help others reach their goals. Don't be unkind, not even to yourself. Let it not be you who judges others for the choices they make in life, when in reality, you do not know the options they had to choose from.

You deserve happiness and a life you're excited about. Don't let anyone make you forget that. At this point in my life, I value consistency, stability, respect, and loyalty above all else. Keep making steady progress, and you'll get there.

Don't be quick to believe everything you hear, whether it's about you or anything else. Lies spread faster than the truth.

Honour God in everything that you do, because when you keep honouring God, the right people will find you. The right opportunities will come across your path. When you honour God, you become a magnet for His goodness. Honour your God, and you will not be ashamed.

What is ahead scares you; what is behind hurts you. Do not forget to look above. He never fails to help and listen to you.

Learn to deal with your past in the right way, ignore what is not necessary from your past, cling to what is memorable from your past, and that can help you make your dream come true, because if you never heal from what hurts you, you'll bleed on people who didn't even cut you. Always remember that at all times.

Learn to be patient. When life feels difficult, it's an opportunity for your patience to grow—so let it. As James 1:2-4 reminds us, you are closer than you think to becoming the person God wants you to be. By His grace, you can overcome challenges and come out stronger and wiser. Stay positive, read God's Word often, trust Him, and remain focused on your path.

When I read Galatians, I feel strong, motivated, and inspired. There are so many reminders that guide us:

Don't live for the approval of others (Galatians 1:10).

Your past does not define you (Galatians 2:20).

Your true worth is in Christ, not your job or education (Galatians 3:27).

Be led by the Spirit, not by your feelings or emotions (Galatians 5:25).

Don't grow weary of doing good; in time, you will reap what you sow (Galatians 6:9).

To live a happy life, ignore the constant chatter of "I heard...," "They said...," or "They say...." Such things only distract and destroy.

Life can be unfair. Many wrongs happen socially and professionally. But we can choose to be kind, loving, and sincere in our homes, workplaces, schools, hospitals, companies—everywhere we go. Let us strive to meet others with good intentions.

True health is more than physical—it's mental, spiritual, and emotional. A loving heart is always healthy. A serving heart is always happy. A caring heart is always strong. The most valuable asset a person can have is a beautiful heart: full of love, ready to listen, and willing to help. No amount of money can match that kind of beauty.

People can be wicked, greedy, and selfish, but our focus should be on nurturing goodness in ourselves and others.

My humble prayer for you today: may God's blessings surround you always. Go with love, peace, and joy.

Alone, we can enjoy life. Together, we can celebrate. Alone, we can smile. Together, we can laugh. This is the beauty of human relationships; we are nothing without each other.

Never feel proud simply because you have something. Remember, someone else made it possible for you to have what you have. Your money, your possessions, and your opportunities are connected to others' efforts. Never look down on anyone. We all have value, but none of us is everything.

Life is the toughest school. You never know what test is next, and you cannot cheat—because your challenges are unique to you. Through it all, keep a positive attitude, trust in God, and keep moving forward.

Chapter 8

Institutional injustices need to stop. We shouldn't blame individuals for everything just because of selfish actions. We shouldn't always insist on having the final say in our workplaces or positions of authority.

If you are a leader in any organisation, whether it's a business, school, hospital, government office, or any other place, remember that the people you work with face different challenges and come from a variety of backgrounds, beliefs, and experiences.

Be a person who can give an ear to listen to people, those that you may despise, have great ideas, and have fantastic opinions that can help you achieve greater heights in whatever you want to achieve.

For example, politicians often seem to dominate every aspect of our lives.

Please respect our rights and stop turning us against each other. We want peace. We are tired of the conflict and pain that comes after every election. Give us a break from all this.

Every day, politics makes people more frustrated and divided. Many of us care about politics and would even serve if given the chance, but we are exhausted. We want to hear something new, not the same old divisive stories. Stop trying to win us over with small gifts that don't make up for years of hardship. While you meet in hotels to plan your next moves, remember that we are not included in those discussions. Bring us ideas that will actually improve our lives, our schools, and our healthcare, which you have neglected. People are suffering while you enjoy lavish meals. Please don't treat us as if we are just part of your celebrations.

If I had the power to rally people against your empty promises, I would encourage them to reject what you offer. But right now, I feel unheard and invisible, and I know you won't listen to me.

Every day, the news and social media are filled with talk about the 'state of the nation,' but it's always about what politicians are doing or arguing about. What does this really mean? Who are they talking to? Who is responsible for the problems we face? I think you know the answer.

Please take a moment to listen and think about what I am saying. I want to share my thoughts. Why won't you listen? I am speaking about our nation, not just myself, because there are many of us. We are the majority.

Poverty is not just an individual problem. It affects groups of people, not just one person. So, who will help us? The government? Politicians? Charities? NGOs? Other countries? If not them, then who?

Chapter 9

Growing up in our village, our father often shared stories about his youth. He said he once killed a huge python in a sugarcane field. It had scared an Indian national, who tried to shoot it but ran away with the gun.

Life was peaceful in the neighbouring villages. Children played together in the common field and shared meals without caring about which family anyone came from. They could even sleep over at friends' homes, and parents didn't mind. It was fun and easy. They went to school as a group and grazed animals together without arguments.

By then, they had almost come from equal backgrounds.

The village elders had an easy job. There were hardly any disputes. Our village was a beautiful place, full of peace, love, and unity.

The neighbourhood was also calm, and they could meet their age-mates across the neighbourhood.

Our village elder was friends with other village elders across the neighbourhood. They reigned for years.

We grew up knowing the chief's family, and we couldn't imagine that another chief from somewhere else.

The chief ruled well and was strong.

Any elders who tried to speak up in the community were silenced by the chief, who did not like competition. He wanted all the respect and the final say in everything. Anyone with a different opinion was removed.

Then trouble came from far away. Intruders tried to invade our villages to steal our healthy crops and livestock. The elders and chiefs united to fight the common enemy. After they won, they decided to choose one leader for all the villages. Our village chief was picked, but when he saw that the neighbouring village had suffered the most, he decided to let their chief lead as a sign of respect. They had paid the highest price.

The neighbouring chief assumed the lead. He led well, calmly, with wisdom. He could meet young men from all the villages, guide them, and teach them the importance of unity against a common enemy.

The new leader collected all the harvests from the three villages for his own village. He even expanded his influence beyond the three villages and became famous throughout the land.

When he became ill, he passed leadership to the next chief, who was from the neighbouring village. Our village chief watched closely and saw that the new leaders had become greedy, and we no longer benefited. So, our chief started to fight for the top position again.

The second leader was tough, strict, and harsh. He did not allow anyone to challenge his power.

One day, our chief called a meeting within our village alone; the elders came together, along with young boys, including my father; the chief's sons were also present. The chief told them, the state they were in as a village was not that good, "...we are being undermined, we are being looted! They are taking everything from us! They are gathering everything for themselves! Look at their village schools; compare with ours, look at their pathways, which are wider and open than ours; look at the houses they are building for themselves; look at their children; look at their water sources! Their village is more lit up compared to ours. We need to fight for our space. We need to fight for our dignity. We need to be free. We need our freedom. We need recognition..."

They tried to remove that chief from power, but they did not succeed.

The chief grew old and became sick, but he did not lose hope. He told his sons and their friends, along with the village elders, to keep fighting for our village's freedom and to work towards gaining power.

The kingpin also had sons, who were also prepared to guard the throne. But they were toddlers. They didn't know much.

The whole community was large, with many capable elders who could have led, but they were never given the chance. They just watched what the ruling chief was doing. Energetic men tried to take power, but they failed and were either removed or silenced for good.

The kingpin was getting older and did not want our chief's son to take over. He called together sons and elders from other villages, including those from the first ruling chief's clan, to plan returning leadership to that clan. But they did not realise that some elders and chiefs from other villages were also angry and unhappy with how things were being run.

Our chief was in the same movement for change as an elder from the far-end village. They defeated them. They took the ruling sword.

The kingpin became friends with our chief's son, who had helped him rise to power. But things did not end well. They broke their promises and agreements. Our chief's son then formed a strong opposition group, which became well known throughout the community.

The son kept trying to become the leader, but he failed several times. Sometimes he managed to defeat the other chiefs and took power by force. Leadership kept shifting between the two villages.

Our chief's son is now an elder in our village. He is the kingpin from our village. He is famous across the neighbourhood. He has friends all over.

But the three villages are still competing for leadership of the whole community.

My father is old now; he is nearly the same age as the chief's son was back then, who is now our village chief and king.

The chief has been through many challenges and learned a lot. He now knows the ways of leadership and is determined to lead. He has promised himself that nothing will stop him this time.

Each of the three villages has produced a leader who is determined to gain power. They all want to rule, no matter what. They have formed alliances and have supporters across the land. Each one is committed to the freedom and progress of their own people.

There are also smaller villages across the land, raising their own sons and daughters who are just as determined to take power if they get the chance.

But then a new threat came to the whole land. It divided the people and disrupted their plans. Some went quiet, while others started to regain their reputation.

First, locusts invaded, then heavy rains caused widespread flooding. As if that was not enough, a deadly disease arrived. It spread quickly and took many lives, making people afraid to gather. Even the chiefs were affected, and some died. The disease stopped the peaceful meetings that used to happen in the villages. With elections for village elders coming up, the disease is still here, and we cannot gather. Older elders who want to lead are now afraid to attend meetings.

People in the three villages are writing warrior songs, but they cannot be sung in public because of the disease. No one wants to risk getting sick. The disease has disrupted government plans and caused social problems. Many have lost their jobs and loved ones. Schools are closed, some for good, and businesses have collapsed. Many young lives have been changed forever, especially for schoolgirls who have become young mothers.

People are suffering at home, afraid of catching the deadly disease in hospitals. Those who do go to the hospital are in pain and misery.

We are suffering from hunger and poverty in our village. Some people blame the chief for letting outsiders come in, bringing the deadly disease with them. He did not want to ruin his friendships with people from outside, so he did not stop them. Because of this, many of us are mourning, have lost jobs, and our businesses have collapsed. Our children are not going to school, and our hospitals are overwhelmed, even using classrooms as temporary isolation centres. The leaders know they are at fault and feel guilty. Health workers are also suffering, but they keep fighting. We pray for mercy.

The chief's officials in different departments are struggling to do their jobs well during these hard times.

The ruling chief has appointed a young man from our village, who is now making his presence felt among the other chiefs' men. Some elders across the land even believe he could one day become the next ruling chief. While that may be true, he has stayed quiet about such ambitions and remains focused on the tasks assigned to him by the chief.

In an exclusive interview with a media outlet, when asked about any interest in political positions, he said, "...from village elder, ward representative, constituency level, county, or even the top seat in the land, none of these positions are vacant at the moment... we will cross that bridge when we reach it..."

He was in charge of education, and things were stable during his time. But now, the current head is going around the village, intimidating and insulting officials in public. I am waiting to ask what his plans are for our education system. Teachers who ask about the academic calendar are being suspended. It's hard to believe. At least he admits that nobody is perfect and says not to trust anyone, not even yourself.

Due to his performance, he was assigned to defence and security matters. There, he is like a lion — when he speaks, people listen, and when he coughs, even the younger leaders step back, knowing they are safe and need not intervene.

The son of our village is gaining fame. The elder, who aims to lead our land, respects him and his work. They have become good friends, though it is still unclear whether he will be officially endorsed when the time comes.

Another son from our village was appointed by the chief to handle legal matters and has successfully tackled major issues. He even challenged the chief himself, exposing illegalities during the chief's election. This caused a daughter from our village to go into exile, and a young man from a neighbouring village was murdered and had his hand cut off — his fingerprints were needed. Another young man from that village was also sent into exile. He is no longer considered a citizen of his birthplace. The land is full of drama, yet we are fascinated by it. Now, two chiefs are sworn in the same village!

The son still holds office, but as he prepares to leave, he has advised the chief to dissolve the community assembly because it has not followed the gender representation rule. The young men and women in the assembly are now supporting leaders from the three main villages, which are considered the most important. These villages are renowned for their strong and educated residents, from whom many experts originate. Our village also has many top thinkers. Lawyers from the neighbouring village are also respected, although some are nervous speakers, and those who are not fluent in English may find it challenging to understand them.

Our kingpin has now gained support from the ruling chief's village against the rival third village, along with some young men from smaller villages, slowly rising beyond our neighbourhood.

Wisdom is not like money; you cannot tie it up and hide it. Our kingpin is wise. He is an elder, respected by other elders in the land, especially the one who leads the Central Organisation of Trade Unions in our community. He does not act recklessly. He speaks with care and understands how things work behind the scenes.

This elder is a close friend of our village chief, supports him, and has access to power across the land. Our chief knows very well that it is better to be loved than feared.

People fear the kingpin from the third large village and do not want him to take power. He was once our chief's right-hand man, learned from him, and then left. Now, he is influencing young men in different villages by giving them small gifts and tools, keeping them busy so they miss out on school or university. Meanwhile, the youth in his own village keep learning and building wealth to stay ahead. The elders are watching him closely, letting him act freely, almost as if they are saying, "Once a calf has drunk milk, it's natural to run around the yard." Other boys keep their distance from him, believing that true friends can share even a drink of water. But he only thinks of himself.

The political wind is blowing across the land. People are forgetting caution over a deadly contagious disease. Elders advise the young kingpin to obey, but he listens to no one. He believes he is always right, calling himself a scientist who interrogates everything, slowly but surely. As a doctor, I can understand the value of questioning, so in that sense, he is correct. But the ruling chief and our chief's men will not accept his ideology because of political differences and his rapid rise to fame.

Who can stop him from ascending to power? He knows where the sword is, how it is guarded, and the way to claim it. He is dedicated, prepared, and believes in himself. He is already making our village chief worried, forcing him to change tactics. Our chief plans to take the sword silently and use it later to threaten the young man, but the boy is fearless. Whether the sword comes before him or not, nothing will stop him this time.

The young kingpin is also uneasy about a new alliance forming between our chief and the ruling chief. Even his own boss intimidates him publicly, yet he has a strong heart and a lion-like courage.

Meanwhile, his village-mate, from the same family, also wants the sword, threatening his rise to power. This rival is powerful, well-known, and supported, capable of undermining him politically. But the elders advising our chief have told him to focus, not to worry about another man's headache. A wise person will always find a way.

Our chief is forming new alliances, gathering powerful men and technocrats in support, and initiating projects to build bridges across the land, which strengthens him politically and increases his fame. The ruling chief understands the sword must leave their village and is preparing a safe place for it, to ensure it is not misused. A community without elders does not prosper, so he listens to them carefully, aiming to leave power with respect and a lasting legacy—regardless of what his right-hand man may desire.

In his second term, our chief has shown he will not tolerate corruption, even among family and close friends. He must appear tough, presidential, and uphold his father's legacy. Despite losing the first two years of his first term to an international criminal case, he earned respect by spearheading a constitutional amendment with his handshake partner.

There were rumours that men from the mountain village planned to eliminate his right-hand man, though they publicly denied it. Who knows the truth? I love my motherland.

Just as the prettiest flowers often have the sharpest thorns, the highest positions of power come with the greatest challenges. We young boys are learning from the elders that respecting them is the path to success. Threats and insults cannot rule a country, so why waste time insulting each other? Reputation and kingdom alike will be lost.

Our chief knows that an intelligent enemy is better than a foolish friend. By publicly shaking hands with his greatest political rival, he sent a message across the community and beyond. In politics—and in life—befriend many, but trust few.

The ruling chief's team is weakening, partly due to his assistant chief and partly because of the new alliance with our kingpin. A house cannot be repaired while its owner is destroying it—let them handle their own problems. We want change in our community, balanced development, and the chance for all villages to hold the sword of power.

Our chief has prepared a bedroom for the next village chief, built a money depot, and created a sports ground where young boys can play and gather. We hope our village ascends to power, clearing paths for schools, universities, industries, and economic growth. There is hope—people who do not kindle their own fire are easy to defeat. Invite boys from across the land, discuss together, but stay focused on the target.

Politics is a dirty game—be ready to be mocked, criticised, or undermined. But you must fight for power; it will not come to you without effort. A big fish requires big bait. Mentor the next generation to guard the sword and understand that equality is difficult, while superiority comes with pain. Go slow when the deal seems too good, and never test a river's depth with both feet.

The government can sometimes turn against its own people. In politics, someone who is your friend today might become your enemy tomorrow. Learn to adapt to different situations. When you are with boys from other villages, be careful how you present yourself in politics. Even a chameleon changes its colour to survive, not to look beautiful.

Do not be quick to point a finger when your neighbour is wrong, yet hide when you are the one at fault. Look closely at the ruling chief—if he is picking out flies from his food, it means he is already full.

Do not fear the sun; rise and become a chief yourself. Let us not become prisoners of hatred by denying others their freedom. Allow everyone to live freely, but fight for what you want quietly and speak only when necessary.

Many boys may watch you fight alone for the sword of power. They may be silent for now, but they are gaining strength, and when they rise, they can overtake you. Chief, make friends with them, but do not let them get too close. A close friend can also become a close enemy.

Remember, it is easier to rise to power than to step down from it. My advice to the boys of our village is: never insult the hunting guide before the sun has set. In our village, mornings are sunny but evenings bring rain. In politics, when you feel you are enjoying success, you should also prepare for hard times.

Patience places a crown on the head. Who does not know that our chief has been patient enough? Let him wear that crown this time. Those watching from afar know that an egg cannot fight a rock—they are waiting for weak points to create a landslide and clear their path.

My father always says: learn as much as you can, even in a foreign land, for knowledge is the one thing you take with you when you die. He jokes too, saying, "Watch your pot when cooking—if you do, your food will not burn."

To my village boys in foreign lands: share meals with strangers, but keep your love for your family. Remember, the oilskin that protects the home is not for outsiders. Bring joy back to our village. Ensure we have water, keep our crops and trees green, and make sure every villager wears a happy face. Fear those silent boys from other villages—their lips beat like a drum.

Bring home the sword of power. Let us grow rich like other villages, for brothers love one another best when they stand equal in wealth. Do not bring misfortune upon others, for in doing so, you only sharpen their wisdom.

Keep trying until you hold that sword. Even a monkey learns to leap from tree to tree by trying often. Carry yourself with good character among other men, for that is how you will earn respect and honour. Do not let our village's beauty turn into ugliness. Without character, ugliness can look like beauty, and beauty can turn into ugliness.

Some may call you a cockroach, but remind them you can still rule the chicken coop—you just need a fox as your guard. Do not be afraid to hire one.

The two kingpins battling for power will never agree. They are like two waterfalls that do not hear each other. Align yourself with one of them, cling tightly, and rise to power—seize the sword.

The ruling chief may already be full, but remember: no matter how full a river is, it still wants to swell. Do not be deceived by fake narratives—us versus them, rich versus poor, hustler versus dynasty. Never forget: the poor man and the rich man rarely play together. Let the fool speak; you listen as a wise man.

Do not grow weary of being whipped many times—the lead cow is always whipped the most. Show respect to the great, so that your own greatness can follow.

They deceive us with their stories. They may change the forest, but they remain the same monkeys. Rain may soak the leopard's skin, but it never washes away the spots. Do not accept bribes; bribery is the enemy of justice.

It may take time for their beautiful people to understand why we support you, even if they think you are ugly. The road will be rough. Some boys say it will be noisy, messy, and full of casualties. Remind them: a smooth sea never made a skilled sailor. Tell them you are ready.

Building bridges will help you cross the river. Stay hidden in the crowd, and the crocodile will not spot you. Earn money, but do not let money rule you.

And above all, listen to the wisdom of elders. That is how you will become a good leader.

A chief's real wealth is their people. We have all seen what the local kingpins have done in our villages — they have turned our neighbours into their subjects. We will no longer accept that. If their sons and daughters want power, let them taste what it's like to be the subject for once. We will not forget what was done to us, however friendly those leaders may seem now.

For too long, we have suffered under the rule of these chiefs. Let them know we are watching, we are aware, and we will demand justice — whatever it takes, for as long as it takes. When they lose power and we take our rightful place, the injustices will be addressed, and those responsible will be held to account. Their families will not escape the consequences of the harm done.

We will replace their cronies in public roles with people from our communities. We are tired of being sidelined. I feel bitter and angry about what has happened — that pain is real. Do not mistake our kindness for weakness. We will not be fooled by sweet words or by people who use charm to divide us.

They have not changed and are unlikely to change. They do not want us to prosper. They do not want our children to go to good schools or for our families to escape poverty. Their aim has been to keep us marginalised — economically, socially and geographically — so that we remain their subjects. We refuse that.

We want better roads, decent homes, good schools and safe workplaces. We want to grow. We are breaking the chains of poverty, political dependency and regional imbalance. We are tired of waiting.

To everyone from our villages — especially the young people — the movement has already begun. Think of the injustices you have witnessed. Put your hand to your heart and say no. Say enough. Stand up wherever you are — at work, in business, in the office — and refuse to accept unfairness. We are all equal; none of us is a visitor in our community. We deserve equal rights and equal opportunities.

Human rights activists and legal channels have tried, but change has been slow and, in many places, conditions have worsened. Stay in the same spirit with me: reject those who destroy brotherhood. We want peace; we do not want gifts that divide us. We must remain united with our neighbours. Do not ask the youth to go door-to-door looking for people's tribe or political loyalty. No one's child should face discrimination. Do not take advantage of our poverty.

Poverty is not permanent. It is not set in stone that we must remain poor. Give us a break — an honest chance to improve our lives.

Elders, please lead us out of this agony. Say no to misery. Let us have decent politics, peaceful campaigns and fair elections. Let people decide for themselves; do not influence or coerce votes.

When we come to power, there will be a lot to put right. We will argue about politics and ideas — that is natural — but we must remain brothers and sisters in our community. Where are the country's think tanks? Speak up. Don't stay silent. Inclusivity cannot be achieved while hatred and division persist. First, let us confront political slavery, marginalisation and hatred; then we can build true inclusion.

I believe — with all my heart — that God hears us. He will help us and bring us victory.

Children learn to walk the way their parents walk. If our fathers were kind and generous, it is wrong to take that kindness as a weakness. Sweet words will not put food on our table. A little steady change — like a little rain filling rivers — will lift us all.

Our anger and grief are real. We are hurting, and at times that pain spills over. Give us a break. You who have enough bread cannot easily see the extent of famine and poverty in our villages.

We have studied your methods and learned from them. We are ready now with ideas for tomorrow's solutions. Do not keep reminding us of the losses you caused for your own greedy gains. Those memories hurt and will not help us move forward. We do not want any more bloodshed.

As young people — and as people with different opinions — we welcome others to join us. We will nurture what benefits the community, even if it grows from difficult beginnings.

To the young men out there: let us speak truth to power without being crude or abusive. Too much argument leads only to quarrels. Keep your dignity. Keep your purpose.

Let us not lose our children because of differences in opinions and ideologies. Children are the true rewards of life.

Let us not be so full of pride that there is no room left for wisdom.

Young people, let us not allow ourselves to become beggars. Our forefathers would not be happy if they woke up and found us in such a state. Let us make our land better than the way they left it.

Refuse to be beggars. Work for yourself and become genuinely wealthy. Do not beg. Do not even appear like one. Even water obtained by begging does not truly quench thirst.

It is impossible to find a person who has everything. But it is possible to find one who enjoys what he has.

Remember, wealth diminishes when it is spent, but learning increases the more it is used.

Let us not suffer sickness when the doctor is available.

Do not be turned against your neighbour.

If they want us to behave, let them behave first. If they want us to stop looting, they must stop looting from us. If they want us to stop fighting, they must stop fighting first. If they want us to be good countrymen, let them be good countrymen first. If they want us to stop hatred, they must end their hatred first. If they want us to stop promoting ethnicity, they must stop it first. Good behaviour must begin at the top.

In times of crisis, the wise build bridges, while the foolish build dams.

Do not think we are all fools. Everyone loves a fool, but no one wants him as a son.

Refuse their cheap politics. Do not fall into their traps. They want to use us. They want to divide us. Stay united. United we stand, divided we fall.

Remember, the skin of the leopard is beautiful, but his heart is not.

They are slowly eroding our morals and values. They are invading us. Stay alert. Do not believe they are kind people. They come only to benefit themselves. Be wise. They befriend us with gifts, but remember: it is the calm, silent water that drowns a man.

Why do they fight so hard for power? A person destined for power does not have to fight for it. Why are they so angry with one another? They are only showing us their own faults.

Let us remain peaceful. Peace is costly, but it is worth every effort.

Do not celebrate the death of an elderly person, for that is like burning down a library. Let us protect our village library, keep it secure, renovate it, and make it a good place for learning.

Collect wealth for yourself, but remember: wealth that enslaves the owner is not true wealth.

People must make several attempts before they succeed. For example, if you are building a house and a nail breaks, do you stop building? No, you replace the nail and continue.

Make use of our elders. Even a king cannot rule without the support of elders.

Do not fear a single smoking stick. It cannot burn.

We have learnt many lessons over a long time. When you lose, you learn more than when you win. Yet we are victors. We have proved this. The one who forgives gains true victory in a dispute.

Let us not behave like an orphaned calf licking its own back. We have elders. Listen to them. Whoever refuses to obey cannot command.

In our youth, let us remember that even in old age, the lion still lives with strength and power.

Be cautious of women from far-off lands who lure us into traps so that their men may rule over us. They say the man is the head of the home, but the wife is the heart. If you marry a monkey for his wealth, the wealth may go, but the monkey remains as he is.

Do not let them use force on us. Remind them that a man who uses force is afraid of reasoning.

Chief, the village bedroom is beautiful, desirable, and admirable. Everyone wants to enter it. But remember, despite the beauty of the moon, sun, and stars, the sky also holds thunder and lightning.

Let our elders remind the chief that a quarrelsome chief cannot hold a village together. Do not allow the chief to keep bad friends who stop him from finding good ones. They have money, but in our village, we do not have as much. Lack of money often means lack of friends. With money at hand, even dogs and goats will claim to be related to you.

Chief, as the captain, do not forget what it means to be a sailor. Always be disciplined. A person without discipline cannot be corrected.

We have cried enough. We do not want to cry anymore. The tears on our faces did not blind us. Instead, they opened our eyes to the future.

They have brought us small gifts to buy our loyalty. But that is still better than nothing. He who receives a gift does not measure its size. We will support you because of the little things you are doing for us. Do not be discouraged. The others are only ashamed of doing nothing. We know their tricks. They have not changed. Because you are for us, they will try to bring you down. But we will stand with you even if they pull you down. A good deed deserves another in return. You have done well for us, and we will repay you.

If given the chance to meet all the young men across our villages and communities, I would explain what it means to suffer in poverty. I would explain what it feels like to encounter poverty face to face. I would say that we need to change our customs, and that begins with changing our kings and leaders.

Let them judge you by the work of your hands. But remember, a strong man's head carries many scars. Do not be afraid. We are with you. We are the majority. We have the power, we have the say, and we will have our way.

It seems you have planted grapes by the roadside. Be ready for the same troubles faced by a man who marries a beautiful woman. If they leave you, just remember this: when a bag tears, the shoulders finally get some rest.

Be strong, because we are with you. We are the majority. Even a tree stands tall because of its roots. At the grassroots, we value your work.

Fellow villager, your own child, though ugly, means more to you than a handsome one belonging to your neighbour. Stand with your son as a village. Be united for once. Do not be divided. That is the enemy's plan. Divide and rule. Leadership does not depend on age. Tell the sons of our village, who work with boys from neighbouring villages, to be wise. Let them be brave enough to embrace the chief. Let them not be brainwashed. Let them not believe false stories.

Around a flowering tree, there will always be many insects. Chief, look around you. How many are we? Know that you are flourishing well. Do not let us down. Talk with them. For us, a good discussion is as valuable as riches.

Those you sheltered politically, who have now defected and try to pull you down, must be reminded of this: you cannot use a wild banana leaf to shield yourself from the rain, then tear it to pieces once the rain has passed. Learning has expanded your soul. No one teaches the paths of the forest to an old gorilla. Let them know that.

Their people say that if the palm of the hand itches, it means great luck is coming. Let them know our palms are itching. The sword is coming to our village. That is our good luck. Bring it home.

Let those boys take a walk. They think they are leading, but no one is following them.

My father told me, loving a king is not bad, but being loved by the king is better.

They gathered riches for themselves, but we gathered knowledge. Now we are better than they are. Victory is ours. We will let them use the same law we have always known: the law is like a spider's web. Only the little insects get caught in it.

They dug a grave for us, but God gave us an emergency exit.

I love politics, I like politics, and yet I also hate politics. Give us a break.

Let us remain a family. A family is like a forest. From the outside, it looks thick and dense, but when you are inside, you see that every tree has its own place.

We know they have money and that they will try to use it to tempt us and hire us when the time comes. Money cannot talk, but it can make lies look true. Our church is falling into this trap. No one is thinking clearly. No one can see. They have all fallen for the lust of money.

We will let boys from other villages come into ours, but we will not let them use us against our neighbours. They will not make us despise old age. All of us, as young men, wish to reach old age, even though we know there is no cure for it.

Chief, do not look where you fell, but where you slipped.

Villagers, let us guard our secrets. Do not share them with unworthy people. That is like carrying grain in a bag with a hole.

I am warning you because I love you. Let us have peace, so that our chief does not need to carry a shield. Let us keep our home affairs off the public square. Tell your boys not to refuse the advice of elders. Without it, they will wander the whole day.

Elders, show us the right way. Let us look at you and see where you sit in old age, and reflect on where you stood in your youth.

A clear-thinking leader is a sign of stability and a force for change in society.

I say to you today, my friends, that despite the difficulties and frustrations of this moment, I still believe we can achieve the changes we desire as a community.

I have reached this conclusion: there comes a moment in life when you must speak for yourself. No one else can do it for you. And you will be held responsible not only for what you say, but also for what you remain silent about.

I refuse to believe that our great vaults of opportunity are empty. There are enough funds. We should not be living in poverty.

Chapter 10

As a young man with most of my life ahead of me, I have chosen to dedicate myself to something eternal and absolute. Not to the little gods that come and go, but to God who is the same yesterday, today, and forever.

I speak fearlessly. Let them know that we are tired of suffering in poverty.

I remind us all that of all the forms of inequality, injustice in health care is the most shocking and inhumane.

Hate harms the hater just as much as the hated. Like unchecked cancer, it corrodes the personality and destroys its vital unity. Many of our inner conflicts are rooted in hate. This is why psychiatrists say, "love or perish." Hate is too great a burden to bear.

We must remember that intelligence is not enough. Intelligence plus character is the goal of true education. Complete education gives not only the power of concentration but also worthy objectives on which to focus.

One of these days, I am going to put my body where my mind is. My mind is uniting our people, preaching peace across our villages, and bringing political sanity to our community. Given the opportunity, that is what I will do.

My father and mother took me to school to get a good education. Now I know that the true function of education is to teach one to think intensively and critically.

As my sufferings increased, I soon realised there were two ways to respond to my situation. I could react with bitterness or transform my suffering into a creative force. I chose the latter.

If I speak of my encounter with poverty, no one should expect an explanation because it speaks for itself. Very few will understand. Those from rich families will always need detailed explanations, but even after many attempts, they may still not understand. Poverty is a foreign word to them. They have never known it, never imagined it, and may not even find it in the dictionaries they use.

Your present circumstances do not decide where you can go; they only decide where you start. Take up one idea, make it your life, think of it, dream of it, live on it. Let your brain, muscles, nerves—every part of you—be full of that idea and set all others aside. This is how you achieve your dreams and success. Believe with all your heart that you will do what you were made to do. Desire success more than you fear failure. Do not let others define you. Do not let the past confine you. Take charge of your life with confidence and determination. There are no limits to what you can do or be. Let thinking be your greatest asset, no matter the ups and downs you face.

I have tried to show that there is no true service of humanity in the profession of medicine and that it can be harmful to mankind. The same is true of politics.

Let each of us try to ensure that through daily prayer, we add something new to our lives, something incomparable. My faith runs far ahead of my reason. I can challenge the whole community and say: we can live peacefully as brothers and sisters, without hatred, ethnicity, or injustice, because we have our good Lord who is, was, and ever shall be with us.

I have concluded that a man is the product of his thoughts. What he thinks, he becomes.

In politics, we often want to associate with those in power, even if it means hating our neighbours because of their ethnic group. We must say no to this kind of brainwashing. A "no" uttered from deep conviction is better and greater than a "yes" spoken just to please or to avoid trouble.

Let us become what we believe ourselves to be. If I believe I cannot do something, I make myself incapable of doing it. But when I believe I can, I gain the ability to do it even if I did not have it at the beginning.

If everyone in politics could say, "I am prepared to die, but there is no cause for which I am prepared to kill," then we would see change.

Let there be a balance of fear. Through that, we will find peace.

Chapter 11

You may find this writing long because I did not have the time to make it short. As I sit and recall my childhood, I reflect on how I began to mature and understand the realities of life. I ask myself many questions, most of which I have never found answers to. Sometimes I feel that life is unfair to some of us. I sit quietly and think, but to what end?

Why do I feel sadness while others are happy? Why is someone joyous and prosperous while I struggle in poverty and misery? Why am I fearful and anxious about my future, while others are full of faith and confidence? Why do some people live in beautiful, luxurious homes while I reside in a slum? Why do some see me as a failure while others are considered great successes? If I stand on a podium to speak, why am I unpopular while others are outstanding and immensely admired?

Why do I toil in life without achieving anything worthwhile while others are geniuses in their work or profession? Why does someone who is poor fail to recover from an illness, while others are healed? Why do immoral or irreligious people often prosper and enjoy good health, while kind and religious people suffer pain in body and mind? Why is one woman happily married while her sister is frustrated and unhappy? I wish I could find answers to these questions.

I have come to understand that I can bring more power, wealth, health, happiness, and joy into my life by learning to access and release the hidden power of my subconscious mind.

As a doctor, when an accident patient is brought to me, I try to understand what may be going on in their mind. I have come to appreciate two very important words in the medical world:

conscious and subconscious. I have taken these words deeply to heart and given them much thought.

In my conscious mind, many things happen. I often get lost in my own imaginary world. I cannot imagine myself as unconscious or entirely subconscious. I think of my mind as a garden. I have a rough idea of its function, and I am the gardener.

I must plant good seeds here — in other words, good thoughts — all day long. I have realised that as I sow in my subconscious mind, so I reap in my body and environment. I must begin now to plant thoughts of peace, happiness, right action, goodwill, and prosperity. I must think quietly and with intent about these qualities and accept them fully in my conscious mind.

I urge you to do the same. Plant wonderful seeds — thoughts — in the garden of your mind, and you will reap a glorious harvest. Your subconscious mind is like soil; it will grow any seeds, whether good or bad. Take charge of your thoughts to bring forth only what you desire. Control your thought process to transform your life.

To change your current condition, change the way you think and picture things in your mind. For example, if you suggest to your subconscious mind before sleep, "I want to wake up at 5 a.m.," it will wake you at that exact time. Convince your mind every night with the idea of perfect health, and your subconscious mind, your faithful servant, will obey.

I see this at work with every unconscious patient I handle. When their thought processes are interrupted, they cannot control their thinking. All I do is help restore their inner self, their thoughts and feelings, by alleviating pain and treating conditions that affect the subconscious mind. I help them return to their "garden," to good thoughts, and to the feeling of health. When this happens, I feel alive; my inner self becomes joyful, my happiness complete, and I feel great. This is the experience I have had.

I now understand why crying makes you feel better, reduces stress, and can help keep the body healthy. Physical health is deeply connected to mental and emotional well-being. If you are in pain or have a chronic illness, it is natural to feel down. Emotions are not just in your head.

Too much anger or stress can damage the body and harm your health. High blood pressure, for instance, is linked to stressful living. The brain even treats social rejection like physical pain. In the same way, losing a limb can trigger phantom pain, which is your subconscious at work. Severe depression can accelerate biological ageing by affecting cells. Feed your mind with good thoughts.

I believe that fitness equals happiness. Exercise, whether running or other intense workouts, releases adrenaline, which can leave you feeling more energetic after the session than before. A good night's rest is also essential. Our brains need around eight hours to recover and consolidate new information to maintain mental health.

When people feel they have no control over events, they tend to see patterns where none exist and believe in conspiracy theories — even in politics. Repeated negative thoughts after a bad event can lead to stress, depression, or mental disorders such as obsessive-compulsive disorder or post-traumatic stress disorder. Some events require family therapy rather than medical treatment.

People with low self-esteem often humiliate others. They genuinely believe their negative opinions are true and unrelated to their own lack of confidence. Humiliating others helps them restore their self-esteem. I have experienced this myself, understanding why friends humiliated me for coming from a humble background.

Finally, moral decisions demand mental effort. Lying, for example, requires constant attention to maintain the falsehood and hide the truth. A person who lies often uses simple sentences and struggles with complex tasks because of the mental load.

A person is not happier because they have a lot of money. They are happier when they have more than their neighbour. People constantly compare themselves with others and feel satisfied if they believe they are superior in some way.

Anger increases people's desire to possess things. They put in more effort to get objects linked with angry faces.

In difficult situations, the more complex a decision is, the more likely people are to leave things as they are.

People under the influence of power behave as though they have suffered a traumatic brain injury. They become more impulsive, less aware of risks, and less able to see things from another person's point of view.

I have come to the conclusion that people generally change for two reasons. Either they have learnt enough that they want to change, or they have been hurt enough that they have to change.

Just wondering, can I say that the people who give the best advice are usually the ones with the most problems?

Often, when people are tense, they forget to notice things even when they are right in front of them.

Try this exercise. Speak to your body. Tell your subconscious mind: your head is relaxed, your thoughts are relaxed, your neck muscles are relaxed, your chest is relaxed, your heart is relaxed, your lungs are relaxed, your abdominal muscles and organs are relaxed, your bladder muscles are relaxed, your thighs are relaxed, your feet are relaxed, your ankles are relaxed. Within a few minutes, you will feel your whole being completely relaxed. Soon after, you may enter a sleepy, drowsy state. If that happens, it means you are in perfect health. What you feed your mind, your mind obeys and carries out.

I do not know if this is what often happens when a person is about to die, especially an adult or an elderly person. I do not know if they speak to their bodies, telling them enough is enough. I do not know if they tell their organs to shut down, their lungs to stop breathing, or their heart to stop beating. Death is a process, and one transforms through its stages. This transformation is physical, and you can observe it. You may see a patient bargaining with angels not to take their life too soon. You may see them in denial. You may also see them finally accept death.

This is what I have come to understand: at the end, the person accepts and speaks to their body, acknowledging the pain caused by illness, and saying, "It is enough, let me rest in peace, without pain, without sickness." Being sick is not pleasant, and I do not want to pass the idea of sickness to my subconscious mind at any time.

I want to be healthy. I want to accomplish my goals and fulfil my purpose in life. I do not want to tell my mind and body that it is time to give up and surrender. My conscious mind does not allow me to speak negatively to my body. It keeps sending signals to keep moving, keep working hard and smart, keep trying and keep pursuing until the very end.

The COVID-19 pandemic has caused great harm. Many people have been deeply hurt. I feel there has been a failure somewhere in our systems of governance. Our health system is not strong enough. Something must be done, and it must be done urgently.

Chapter 12

Working in a hospital that was chosen to be a centre for coronavirus patients was a nightmare. Things there were not in good shape at all. Everything was in a mess.

What we saw on television, heard on the radio, and read on social media about the deadly, contagious disease was completely different from what we were experiencing inside the hospitals. The reality, especially in the one where we worked, was the exact opposite of what was being shown.

Every day, we listened to senior officials in the health sector proudly declaring how well-prepared the country was for the pandemic. They spoke about how great the plans were for protecting frontline workers. We saw news reports, heard radio announcements, and read social media updates claiming that personal protective equipment (PPE) had been distributed across the nation, especially to hospitals handling confirmed cases.

It all sounded reassuring—until you saw what was happening on the ground. We were there, treating patients face to face, often without any form of protection.

The World Health Organisation (WHO) issued clear guidelines on how to protect ourselves, the most important being the use of face masks. Yet, our system was rotten from top to bottom. Don't think that the so-called "COVID millionaires" exposed in the media were only those in high offices. The corruption and greed went much deeper. At the grassroots level, the situation was far worse—tragic and heartbreaking.

Healthcare workers were left unprotected. Even basic face masks were unavailable for a long time. And when they finally arrived, the supply was too small. Within the facility, loopholes allowed these masks to be stolen or diverted for personal gain. Those in charge didn't care about us—the junior staff who were the most exposed.

When masks arrived, we saw them only on the faces of those sitting comfortably in offices. They wore them as they relaxed on their chairs, sipping tea and eating meatballs, while we were out there handling patients barefaced.

As junior staff, nobody cared about our safety. We were expected to show up, to handle patients, and to keep the hospital running. By then, testing kits were scarce, and only one centre handled the tests. Results took days to return. In the meantime, we kept attending to patients—without PPE.

The virus spread fast. Many people contracted it, some became gravely ill, and others died. Still, we didn't receive the proper protective gear.

Cartels were everywhere. Senior staff who had access to the limited PPE hoarded them for their families and friends, or even sold them outside for profit. They did not care about their colleagues' lives. I don't know how rich they became, but I am sure they are not at peace knowing that healthcare workers died because of their greed. Woe to those who kept what was meant to save lives. I have no kind words for them—my conscience will not let me.

In the wards, we continued working as usual. Patients suffered terribly. I have not been in the medical profession long enough to grow numb to pain. Watching patients in agony and pretending everything was normal was impossible for me.

My friends and I attended to every patient, no matter the condition. I could not stand by and see someone begging for help while I did nothing simply because I lacked PPE. I couldn't let patients suffer and die when I knew I could help.

My name became known throughout the facility. Even patients who had passed through my hands remembered me. But many others were left unattended.

We were a team of interns—young, inexperienced, and alone. The senior staff, though on the payroll, stopped reporting to work. No one punished them. Some even called from home to check if we were at work, while we risked our lives every day.

A few kind people cared enough to share the limited face masks with us whenever they could. At the height of the infection, a frontline healthcare worker could be forced to use a single surgical mask for a week—sometimes even two. If you were lucky, you might get another one after three days.

In the beginning, we focused only on a few symptoms—fever, cough, and difficulty in breathing. But not all COVID-19 patients showed these signs. I believe our biggest mistake from the start was the narrow focus on temperature. Everywhere, even in the main centres for confirmed cases, we relied too heavily on this one symptom.

The rise of thermoguns was everywhere. They were used well, misused well, not used well, and, most importantly, they misled us all.

In many cases, later confirmed, had already spread across the country simply because we focused on one symptom. The severity of the disease varied in every individual, depending on one's immunity, which became a major factor in how it spread.

Groups of patients would come for triage. Their temperatures were taken, and they were asked a few questions — whether they had travelled abroad, had contact with someone who did, or had difficulty breathing, coughing, or other respiratory symptoms. Yet in most of them, even those already infected, the temperature was normal.

Because testing capacity was low, only those with severe symptoms were tested. The rest — the silent, asymptomatic carriers — went undetected. They moved freely among the public, infecting others, including unprotected healthcare workers. The spread was unstoppable.

We fed our minds with one dangerous belief: if your temperature is normal, you are safe. You could go anywhere — gatherings, meetings, markets, schools, even hospitals.

Coughing is a reflex; it can happen for many reasons. But try coughing in a public vehicle during the pandemic. You would be thrown out, or everyone would jump out and run far away from you.

We were made to believe that corona meant coughing. We were made to believe that wearing a mask meant you were safe. We were made to believe that a normal temperature meant you were disease-free. Who misled us? Whose fault was this?

I don't know what the studies about the virus will reveal, but for now, most of us remain in the dark.

The public tends to believe every word spoken by healthcare workers, especially about protection and safety. Yet schools were closed, curfews imposed, and lockdowns enforced — and still, infections and deaths kept rising each day.

I believe we also misled ourselves. Sanitising our hands and boarding a matatu doesn't mean we cannot infect others. It's an airborne disease. Not all masks sold in our markets protect against the virus.

At the beginning, mask prices were so high that most people couldn't afford even one. Now, we cry out because PPEs are rotting in the country's medical supply stores. The big fish are involved — what can you do? You can shout, but eventually, you'll grow tired and fall silent.

Don't even ask about buying a mask daily. Poverty is a major reason the disease spread so widely. People couldn't afford masks — some couldn't even afford a meal. Businesses shut down, jobs were lost, and the economy collapsed.

People died because someone failed to protect a frontline worker — a worker who could have saved others and slowed the spread.

Huge, expensive machines were bought using donations meant to help manage the disease. Funds allocated to fight the pandemic enriched a few. They took advantage of tragedy and turned it into profit.

The political class — only a few cared. Most hid away, watching from their comfort zones as ordinary Kenyans suffered.

Hospitals have become places of silent misery. The government must do something for its healthcare workers.

Imagine sitting in a consultation room in a public health facility. A patient walks in — well-dressed, looking healthy, with only a mild headache. Across the table sits a doctor who hasn't eaten for three days, wearing a torn shirt, faded trousers, cracked shoes, and a wrinkled lab coat. The doctor looks nothing like the patient's idea of a healer.

Some patients doubt they are even in the right place. Some walk out without saying a word. Others speak, but without faith that they'll be helped. And in the doctor's mind runs a single thought — maybe, just maybe, this patient will offer a few shillings for supper.

This became a trend. Even those who were not struggling financially developed the habit of taking money from patients—a practice commonly known in hospitals as scoring. It was thought to be a behaviour of junior staff, but in truth, the ones deeply rooted in it were often the seniors and those in offices. Everyone wanted a share of the same patient.

In my consultation room, I wanted a little cash from the patient. Someone in the laboratory wanted something too. Go to the X-ray or ultrasound departments, and you will find others waiting for their turn to "score." It wasn't always about exploitation, but what the patient was supposed to pay to the facility ended up being pocketed by individuals instead.

When the patient returned with their results, they had to bribe the guard to get quick access to the doctor's room for interpretation and a prescription. Even at the registration desk, they were already "scored." They might be told they would receive an NHIF form—even if they were not NHIF members—so they could get free services. But for that "favour," they still had to give a small amount.

Now, when a healthcare provider saw a patient carrying an insurance form, the thought was, I can't get anything from this one; let me hurry with them and wait for the next patient who might have some cash for me. This cycle repeated in almost every department the patient visited. In the end, the patient did not receive the quality healthcare they deserved.

Who is to blame? You can help me answer that.

The patient might have received services almost free of charge—but what kind of services were those? Even those with insurance began preferring to pay in cash, hoping to get at least decent care, though often rushed through, so more patients could be attended to, and more money could be collected.

All this happens because the salaries of healthcare workers are meagre. There are constant strikes. People grow tired of repeating the same demands: salary increments, promotions, and the implementation of Collective Bargaining Agreements (CBAs). Yet the government and those responsible turn a deaf ear.

As a result, "scoring" becomes a desperate survival tactic in a harsh economy and difficult working environment.

Patients with money get the best care and the most attention—because they can pay for it. But what about those who cannot afford it? The government is supposed to take care of them, yet does it really do so? It should, by employing enough healthcare workers and paying them well. But that remains a daytime dream in our country.

We are obsessed with politics. We have even politicised our healthcare.

The government must act. Those responsible for the health sector must do their duty. And those sitting in offices doing nothing—fire them! Fire them! Just fire them! They are not doing justice to the people.

We cannot allow someone who can barely afford a single meal in three days to die simply because they cannot pay for healthcare. This must stop.

Let us not enslave our minds into thinking health is all about money. Your health should never become a money scam for anyone's gain. Let us cleanse our healthcare system.

When things got worse, we took to the streets. We marched to the Ministry of Health headquarters to demand our pay.

Still, there were many good senior staff in the facility. Those I worked with were kind—especially in the wards and outpatient department. I salute you all. The consultants were patient and generous. They taught us well, guided us carefully, and allowed us to practise both what we knew and what we didn't, under their supervision. Keep being good to your juniors.

We were given a wonderful opportunity. We learnt a lot, practised a lot, gained many skills, and performed many procedures. Today, I sit in my own hospital—though still in a dream—but with gratitude for all the exposure and lessons, both good and bad.

Some taught us valuable clinical and surgical skills—how to manage medical, surgical, obstetric, gynaecological, and paediatric emergencies. We truly appreciate that. But there were also those who taught us how to exploit patients. To them, too, I say thank you—you helped us survive then.

To any patient who might have fallen into our hands during that time and felt we failed you, I am deeply sorry. It was never right, but it was our way of surviving. Please forgive us. I wish you good health and healing in abundance.

The management then didn't seem to care—and if they did, I cannot understand how all this was allowed to continue. Anything was permitted, as long as it brought money out of the patient's pocket. Patients were even sent for unnecessary tests, just to make sure the cartels had something to share at the end of the day.

When the contagious disease was at its peak, the funds for combating it in our facility were increased. The interns, together with other staff members, were assigned to the screening areas every day. Even then, we were working in highly risky conditions, most likely to contract the virus in those zones. There were not enough PPEs, not even simple surgical masks. We had to protest for them. We had no say, no office to take our complaints to. Our in-charge tried several times to raise the issue but grew tired—

there was nothing more he could do. Yet, like sheep heading to the slaughterhouse, we kept working.

We were promised risk allowances for serving at COVID-19 screening points. That never happened. Still, we took our shifts with enthusiasm and hope that whatever little we would receive could at least help us with food or clothing as we continued to serve. That promise remains unfulfilled—a hollow echo of what was assured. I still wonder whether those responsible ever think about the allowances we were never paid.

Later, we were deployed to different lower-level health centres to familiarise ourselves with the Universal Health Coverage (UHC) programme—a presidential initiative and one of the "Big Four Agenda" goals he aimed to achieve before the end of his term. We requested COVID-19 tests before moving to our new workstations because we were coming from the epicentre. We feared we might unknowingly carry the virus and infect others. None of that happened. If this deployment occurred across the country, then perhaps we now understand the origin of many subsequent infections.

To those who contracted the virus from us while we attended to you, we are deeply sorry. But what I still cannot find words for is how to speak to someone who lost a family member, a friend, a lover, or a relative because of this.

For a long time, we kept receiving daily COVID-19 updates. Yet, I kept wondering—how prepared were we as a nation to curb the spread when even protecting the healthcare workers, those entrusted with fighting the virus, was such a challenge?

Correct me if I am wrong, but how can an army be sent to a battlefield without weapons? It is like sending them to die. That is what healthcare workers—the frontline soldiers—were asked to do. Go and die first for us. Once you are gone, the rest of the public will face it next.

What pains me most, and I do not know when that pain will fade, is remembering how patients were left unattended and given poor-quality services simply because healthcare workers were not properly protected. Some patients died, not necessarily from the virus, but from a lack of proper care.

I remember one moment that broke me completely. I cried quietly in the ward, though no one noticed. A middle-aged woman was on oxygen support for a medical condition and chest infection. Just moments before she died, she said to me, "I am tired, doctor. Let me rest. I am tired of breathing. Let me rest." She was struggling terribly to breathe. She ate her lunch quickly, as if she knew it would be her last meal, as though she was racing against time—her time had come.

I adjusted her oxygen mask again, but she removed it and repeated softly, "I am tired, let me rest." Then she went silent. Slowly, by her side, she started gasping—and she died. The pain still lingers in me.

When her daughter came in a few minutes later, she found a nurse, a colleague, and me standing beside the bed after our failed attempts to resuscitate her mother. From the look on my face and the silence around, she immediately knew something was wrong. I couldn't bring myself to tell her. She looked at me and said, "Doctor, you did your best. It's not your fault. Let her rest." Only a few moments later did she break down in grief. She had comforted me when it was I who should have been comforting her. May her soul rest in peace.

I later shared the experience with a senior nurse in the department. She asked me just one question: "For how long will you keep crying for every patient you lose? How many will you cry for? Those who die in your hands—this may be the first, but it will not be the last. Take heart. It has happened, and it may happen again. That is what being a doctor means."

I remember that afternoon well. I worked, but not effectively. When I reached home, my wife asked why I looked so low, so tired and moody. I told her everything. I felt as though I had lost a part of myself. At that time, I had not yet faced many such cases.

One day, I found a colleague crying in the nursing room. She had just lost a patient she had been monitoring and caring for over several days. It hurt deeply. I often wonder if the relatives who lose a patient truly understand how painful it is for the doctor or nurse who fought to keep that life going.

I have learnt that the greatest act of kindness and humanity I can offer is to ease pain, to relieve suffering, and to help my patients return to health. That I will continue to do—with God's help. Amen.

Working in the emergency room has brought many lessons. Some experiences were good learning opportunities, but others were terrifying and left scars. A patient could arrive, and before we even discovered what was wrong, they would pass away while we tried desperately to stabilise them.

There is no pain or despair quite like a failed resuscitation. To hold a person's life in your hands and still lose them—it breaks something inside you.

Patients who are sick or in pain are willing to do anything to get help, especially when the doctor assures them it's necessary for their recovery, even when they cannot afford it. For this reason, many patients are exploited—not only in public hospitals, where this is common, but also in private ones. Some facilities have been exposed for the same reason: exploiting patients through unnecessary tests, investigations, scans, procedures, and medications, all to drain them financially. They milk every possible source—insurance, savings, loans—until there is nothing left. When the money is gone, the patient is suddenly referred elsewhere, under the excuse of "financial constraints." God have mercy on us.

In some facilities, patients are left unattended until death takes its course—simply because they lack money. You may not be a stranger to such stories, or perhaps you have even experienced it yourself.

Our healthcare system is rotten, if I may say so. It may sound strange to hear a professional condemn their own institution, but I must speak the truth—if only to bring a little sanity and humanity back into the system.

Chapter 13

Mumbai, India, in one of the referral hospitals.

It was a beautiful morning, calm and cool. The day had begun as usual. Everything seemed to be running smoothly. Patients streamed in from the gate to the consultation rooms. The flow was steady, the atmosphere peaceful.

The management team was on its regular morning rounds, moving through each department, checking if things were running well. If they spotted a problem, they fixed it quickly and carried on. By mid-morning, once the rounds were done, the managers returned to their offices. And that was when the real picture of the hospital came to life.

Each worker took their position. The daily routine began—but not the one written in policy. Everyone had a mission: to make money from the desperate patients. Some patients were stopped right at the gate, others at the registry, and many more in the waiting area. Soon, the place turned chaotic. No one was spared. It became serious business. No one wanted to be interrupted or questioned. The mission was clear—money first, service later. It didn't matter what kind of service was given or who gave it.

The helpless patients, with no other choice, gave in to the system.

At the main gate, the security guard would ask where the patient was going and what service they needed. Then he would make a quick call to a health worker with whom he had an arrangement: "Send me a patient, and I'll share a little of what I get." When the patient reached the person on the other end—sometimes a nurse, sometimes support staff—they were welcomed and asked about their problem.

Then came the next deal. To avoid the long queues, the patient was told to pay a small amount directly to the staff member. In return, things moved faster. Samples for lab tests were taken hurriedly in poor conditions, and the patient was told to wait for results. If imaging was needed, the health worker would again take cash, walk over to the imaging department, and arrange a quick, secret transaction.

When the results were ready, the patient was called privately and examined. Now it was time for medicine. Drugs were given right there in the consultation room, not from the pharmacy. These medicines came from medical representatives who visited daily, each trying to get their company's products sold. To win over health workers, they offered gifts, cash, or even free lunches at nearby hotels.

The patients were persuaded to buy these medicines directly, often at inflated prices—though sometimes, depending on the person, at a cheap rate. Through it all, not a single rupee reached the hospital's account. Every bit was shared among health workers, support staff, and even security personnel.

It was a sorry state indeed.

Some patients even paid the guards manning the queues to skip the line and see a doctor sooner. Others had to "arrange" with pharmacy staff to get medicines without receipts. Many support workers used their NHIF cards to collect drugs from the pharmacy, then resold them to patients through the same health workers.

The NHIF office itself joined in. They would offer forms to patients—even those who weren't members—for a fee of one thousand shillings. That form, they said, would let the patient get free treatment afterwards. Many believed it was worth it.

So the patients went through the full process: consultation, tests, medicines, and went home feeling well treated. But not a single rupee from them went into the hospital's account. When the hospital later tried to claim from NHIF, they couldn't—because those patients were never real members.

Even in the wards, patients had to dig into their pockets to pay for small favours.

And so, day after day, the hospital bled silently—corruption thriving where healing was meant to happen.

Take, for example, the maternity wing. For a patient to receive a service such as imaging requested by a health worker, an informal arrangement is often made—either with the health worker or a support staff member—to ensure faster service at the ultrasound department. The cash must be handed over first to an individual. Remember, maternity services in our country's public health facilities are meant to be free and fully funded by the government. We have programmes like Linda Mama and Beyond Zero that are supposed to take care of pregnant mothers in public healthcare facilities.

In outpatient clinics, if a patient needs surgery or any other procedure, and plans to use the NHIF card to pay, they are often told that the process will take too long or that NHIF will not cover certain procedures. This is said to convince the patient to pay out of pocket so the procedure can be arranged faster. Some patients, frustrated by the delay, agree. Once this happens, the service provider contacts the records department in the specialised clinics to make faster bookings for that patient, and they share the cash. The patient gets the service quickly, but at a fee. The surgeon in the theatre, or even the consultant, may have no idea about these arrangements because the patient is often instructed to remain silent about them.

If a patient was supposed to wait six months for a service due to full bookings but is told they can pay a little money to receive it immediately, many agree. Some have been returning to the hospital for months, waiting for a minor procedure that never happens, until they finally give in and pay. These small payments help some junior staff make ends meet—sometimes it's the only way they can afford even a single meal.

But should it really be this way? Should we normalise these kinds of shortcuts and backdoor arrangements?

Some senior staff discourage this behaviour because they know what goes on, especially in the outpatient department. But then again, what is the difference between a junior staff member asking a patient for a small payment to get faster service and a senior staff member referring the same patient to their own private clinic, where they will pay much more? Both acts serve personal gain and self-interest. How can they condemn the juniors while doing the same thing themselves?

And if one concludes that these acts in the outpatient clinics are illegal, what can be said when even the top management—the hospital administrator and the medical superintendent—are involved in similar shady arrangements?

For instance, in one city hospital in Kampala Luganda, the hospital administrator reportedly works with the head of security to siphon money from medical representatives. Each representative must pay one thousand shillings to the head of security, who then passes the money directly to the administrator. This payment allows the representatives to enter the facility and talk to health workers about their company's products. As a result, these representatives are also forced into local deals with healthcare workers, offering free drug samples to win their favour and secure prescriptions for their medicines.

In the end, it is always the patient who suffers the most.

Before you rush to condemn the hospital administrator for these actions, remember this is only part of the story. We have not even spoken about how he or she mistreats the nurses and other healthcare workers. This has created deep resentment among the staff. The medical superintendent, who is the hospital's overall head, is also not innocent. He, too, is involved in these questionable dealings for personal gain. The money collected from the billing office, even the small amounts from the NHIF office, somehow finds its way into pockets we cannot trace—no one is sure whether it ever reaches the hospital account.

Let us not even begin with the charges relatives have to pay for mortuary services. That money too disappears into someone's belly. You can treat these as allegations if you wish—it is up to you.

The social work office, which is meant to help patients who cannot afford their hospital bills, is also caught in the web. This is especially true in NGO-run, public, faith-based, and private hospitals that are financially capable of offering waivers. Some of the staff there take advantage of desperate patients, particularly those with large bills. They promise to arrange a waiver in exchange for a small payment made directly to them.

Think about it—these are patients who underwent surgery where the surgeon, assistant surgeon, anaesthetist, theatre nurses, and supervisors all worked tirelessly to save a life. The consultants reviewed them daily, nurses cared for them through sleepless nights, and lab staff conducted endless tests. Yet all their hard work goes unpaid. The patient gives a small bribe, is discharged quietly, and walks free. Tell me, how can a hospital survive like this?

It gets worse. Some junior staff have secret arrangements with the security team to help patients leave without clearing their bills. I have even heard of health workers using their own cars to sneak patients past the gate unnoticed.

To the patient, it feels like relief, an escape from debt. But many of them are not truly unable to pay. They are lured and pressured into these deals. Ironically, some end up paying more than they would have through the proper process. It is corruption disguised as help.

I see my colleagues doing these things, and I feel helpless. It is not entirely their fault—they are driven by hardship and desperation.

Even some nurses, though not all, take part. They look through files, find patients already discharged by consultants, and make their own secret arrangements for early release.

There are also special deals with outside facilities offering CT scans, MRIs, and advanced lab tests. Health workers refer patients there in exchange for commissions. In the worst cases, patients are sent for unnecessary imaging—not because it's needed, but because it earns someone extra money. The requester writes their name and phone number so that their commission can be sent directly to them.

Imagine a patient in severe pain being sent outside the hospital for a test that could have been done in-house, cheaper, quicker, and more accurately. They wait in long queues, wasting time and money, just to fill someone's pockets. Is that justice?

Then there is the medical examination office. Patients seeking reports—for school admission, job applications, or medical fitness—are supposed to pay six hundred shillings: five hundred for the service, one hundred for registration. Yet they are often charged up to one thousand dollars to get the same report. Even students who can barely afford it are exploited.

Now tell me, if you have ever had to get a medical report from a public facility, did you go through proper tests? Or did you just answer a few questions, pay something small, and walk out with your report? Be honest with yourself.

Who is to blame—the one offering the bribe, or the one accepting it? Both are part of the same chain. Corruption has taken root in every corner of our society.

So let us not only point fingers at the political elite. It is easy to condemn leaders, especially those from the opposing side. But the truth is, corruption lives within us all.

Stop corruption—start with yourself! Stop giving or accepting bribes. Do not rush to judge others for being corrupt just because they are public figures. Judge yourself first.

Imagine this: a doctor sits in the consultation room. A patient walks in with laboratory and radiology results. Where was this patient seen before? Why didn't they return the results to the person who requested them? Sometimes, the person who ordered the tests could have been a support staff member or someone at the registry. If the doctor isn't kind enough to check and interpret the results or give a prescription, the patient may be sent back to the one who requested the test.

If that person happens to be a casual worker in the facility, they might approach a junior or senior staff member, explain the situation, and request that the patient be attended to. Everyone in the system knows about these arrangements. Meanwhile, the patient—already miserable, desperate, and in pain—has to go through humiliation, confusion, and endless waiting, forced to comply with whatever system is in place.

Sometimes patients wait for hours because the very first person they met at registration referred them to a particular provider they have an "arrangement" with. Even if that provider is busy or not around, the patient must still wait. If you've ever experienced this, you know how real it is.

This is what happens to almost every patient seeking healthcare. No one is spared. Each individual in the chain has their own daily targets to meet. And when something goes wrong, cover-ups begin. If one case backfires, a chain of cover-ups follows—from the very first person involved to the last department. Even the offices where complaints are supposed to be reported are part of these corrupt arrangements. How can they punish anyone when they themselves are part of the problem?

Healthcare workers' unions do their best to fight for members' rights—better pay, allowances, and safe working environments. But some members still find shortcuts to make ends meet.

This cycle will never stop if young professionals like me continue following the wrong examples we see around us. I refuse to lose my morals.

But what if the environment becomes too hard to survive in? Will I also fall into the same corrupt system?

No—I choose to do what is right. I choose to deliver safe, quality, and affordable healthcare to all. I choose not to be corrupt. Do not pressure me into unethical acts when you come to my hospital or any institution where I work. I will not corrupt my mind. I will not ruin my values. I will build the right skills and knowledge to serve people with integrity.

It is sad that when top officials in hospitals engage in corruption, juniors become the scapegoats. When a junior is caught doing what everyone else does, the blame falls on them—not because of what they did, but because it threatens to expose the seniors' involvement. It is deeply unfair.

During my entire internship, I saw this happen every single day. What I've shared here is only a glimpse of one day's reality. You don't want to imagine how long this has been going on.

And it's not just one hospital. Other facilities across the county face the same. Colleagues, friends—everyone shares similar stories. This is what's happening across the country.

Who will stand up for our citizens—our innocent patients? They come to us in pain, in agony, and in desperation. Yet the very people who are supposed to heal them end up exploiting them.

Visit private clinics and specialist hospitals and see for yourself. In most cases, the person attending to you isn't even the specialist. They're someone from the same profession but without that particular specialisation, hired because they're cheaper to maintain. The facility takes full payment for specialised care but provides something else.

Still, one thing remains certain: the personnel employed are often well-trained and capable. They provide nearly the same service the specialist would have offered. But the deception—charging for what is not truly given—is part of the larger corruption we must end.

I am not speaking from outside the profession. I am speaking honestly, from within. I am not spying, nor am I trying to expose anyone. My purpose is to share the truth—that our healthcare system is failing and on the verge of collapse. Let us give every client the service they truly deserve, the same quality they expect and are willing to pay for.

If there are not enough specialists, then employ more. Be ready to pay them well for the vital work they do. Let us not be mean or greedy.

But if this happens, how many people will lose their current jobs? Not only in healthcare, but in every sector. Can this really be done? The answer, sadly, is no—and we all know the reasons why.

When we visited the Ministry of Health, we were allowed into the top offices. What we saw in the waiting rooms was deeply disappointing. Old, torn chairs. Dirty walls. Faded papers in files, in this modern age of technology and information systems. These offices need transformation. Let us not build beautiful structures that shine from the outside but are a mess within. I believe the boss's office is neat, clean, and beautifully decorated with expensive seats and furniture. But what about the visitor who never makes it past the waiting area or reception? What impression do they leave with? Let us sanitise our offices—especially top government offices like the Ministry. They deserve better.

And it is not just that one office. There are many others. Because these are public offices, let us make them look decent. Stop looting funds into personal accounts abroad while neglecting even the appearance of the very workplaces you sit in.

These problems exist across all sectors. A colleague once shared his experience from one of the top offices in Uganda—the National Social Security Fund (NSSF) building, known as Uzee House. He told me about a support staff member there who was nearly fired. A co-worker went to great lengths to protect him by forging medical reports and appointment cards to prove that he had been ill and under treatment. The documents were official and well-stamped with a hospital seal—but all of it was fake.

The person who arranged it only wanted to help the old man. He wasn't mentally sharp and barely understood what was happening. He worked in the office, but his role was unclear—probably a messenger or support staff. Still, these kinds of arrangements are deeply rooted in every department and sector of our nation.

Corruption has taken root in our hearts. No one believes that success can be achieved without it.

Those forged documents for the old man's case are probably still on file. And I cannot believe that the person who made them acted alone. It is likely that those in higher positions also played a part. The information suggests that even the boss ordered it. The old man didn't know who wanted to fire him or who saved him. The medical reports convinced the office that he was genuinely unwell for three or four months, attending hospital appointments and counselling sessions—but it was all on paper.

Let us change. We can stop such behaviour.

My colleague told me it was quite an experience sitting in that big public office. The seats were large, soft, and made of fine leather. He had never imagined sitting on such luxury so soon. He was even taken to the staff restaurant for lunch—big fish, kienyeji, and ugali. Afterwards, they went to a nearby supermarket for fruit and yoghurt. He said it was a wonderful experience.

I share this in simple language to show what truly happens inside our offices. How I wish I could visit more top offices in our country and see for myself what goes on there.

I once visited the Public Service Commission headquarters in the CBD. The story there was no different. The mission is the same everywhere—scrambling for easy money.

At the reception, so much happens. To get the service you need, you must earn some favour. You cannot reach the office you want without going through the usual routine. They will tell you to wait for a few minutes while they "pass the message." During that time, you are expected to offer something. If you do not, the reply will soon come: "The boss is busy and cannot attend to you today." Then you are told to come another day. And you keep waiting, over and over, until you finally give up—simply because you are not part of the arrangement.

Even the security checks at the main gate reveal the truth: some are barely done at all, while others—people who might not even look suspicious—are subjected to the most thorough scrutiny. It is not about whether they appear to be a threat. No! The bottom line is money. Do you look like someone who can pay? Or are you just here for justice?

Even in our courts, where we expect justice to be served freely, you must pay top lawyers to get that justice. Advocates will tell you: everything comes at a price. You cannot expect me to pay for services at your office and then assume you will be spared when I need something in return. The same rules apply here—our institutions operate on similar arrangements. Corruption exists at every level, however small it may seem. Corruption is still corruption.

The root of this problem is low socioeconomic status. People are struggling in poverty. The rich who engage in corruption may do so out of greed, but the real poor are suffering because of survival. They could tell you stories that you wouldn't believe because you've never experienced true poverty. You've never felt what it means to sleep hungry, to be locked out by a landlord. You can't imagine it if you live in multi-million-dollar mansions, drive luxury cars worth millions, often bought with stolen money. Very few of them earn their wealth from honest hard work.

I went to the National Transport and Services Authority (NTSA) headquarters just to apply for a smart card driving licence. The arrangements at the gate were obvious. Follow the procedures, bring the documents—but access to the offices is reserved for those who "look worthy," those who appear able to pay. Everyone else? You pay online, wait decades for an appointment, and hope they eventually communicate. They exploited the pandemic, but it's never really about the pandemic: you have to pay at least one thousand shillings to get services at NTSA offices.

Why are we so entrenched in these corrupt practices? Who planted these ideas in our minds? Who made us believe that favours must be exchanged for every service in this country?

The same arrangements exist in the best government driving schools, where I trained. A little cash can get you through the test—even if you don't know how to move the vehicle forward or backwards. And these are likely the majority of the drivers on our roads, which is why accidents happen every day. We need to clean up our driving schools—but corruption does not stop there. The same practices are mirrored in top offices.

Take our police service, for example. I once participated in a recruitment exercise. Chances were being sold to those with cash, lining the pockets of officials. While some candidates went through rigorous physical exercises and checks, others bought their way in. Big bellies with briefcases full of money walked into offices, while letters went to people who were not even part of the exercise, not even from the localities. Money speaks.

Who has bewitched us as a nation?

In schools, colleges, and campuses, certain arrangements quietly persist. They happen. Students offer favours, others exchange their bodies, all in the pursuit of some advantage—whatever it may be.

If you want to see how deep these arrangements run, look at the media. To get your story aired, you must either have connections or present something so crucial that it guarantees high viewership. Without such arrangements, speak and see who listens: no one. You are a nobody. Who are you if you cannot pay for a service?

I am not saying we should not pay for services we use—the processes involved matter—but we need sanity, fairness, and integrity in them.

Think about your job search. Whatever your career or profession, what was your experience? Were you asked to give something to gain favour? Some of us might be lucky, but that doesn't mean these acts don't happen.

In every office, institution, company, or organisation, we know such things occur. So why can't we stop them? Be the person to start the change—the move to bring sanity, integrity, and transparency. Be the one to ignite the long-awaited revolution. Rise up. Shine. You are not alone. Everyone is waiting to see who will start the conversation. That person can be you. Press that button. Start the move. Stop waiting for someone else—they are all afraid.

Senior workers are quick to condemn juniors, yet they are often worse. The juniors learned it from them. They are the teachers, the role models—they taught by example. We followed your teachings; why condemn us now? Condemn yourself first!

I remember one senior staff member who approached me: "You are kind, willing to learn, and doing an amazing job. We like your service. We will recommend you. But your flaw is this: you have learned everything—both good and bad." I laughed, but his words stayed with me. He was giving me a warning, a lesson from experience. In the public hospital, he does not exploit patients. Yet in his private clinic, he syphons money from the same patients. And I ask: what difference does it make?

I chose to follow the right path: always do the right thing, always give your best, in everything you do.

In these arrangements, the caution is to channel siphoned money through accounts that cannot be traced, avoiding direct evidence. These practices exist everywhere. People have foreign accounts, moving money under the guise of international business. Corruption cases go nowhere because the trails are like cobwebs—impossible to follow. Investigations never end.

Before shouting about public officials looting funds, examine yourself. How much have you taken from customers in your small business? If you have, you lack the courage to call anyone else corrupt. Keep quiet.

Chapter 14

A very unique and haunting experience in the emergency room was this: on almost three occasions, I had to watch a patient die on the bed, not knowing what to do—simply witnessing their death by their bedside.

A very sick elderly person, especially a man, might say to a doctor, "Doctor, I need to go to the washroom to urinate." Once they are allowed to get up from the bed, they may never return. Death takes them. I do not know what happens in those moments, and even to this day, I cannot fully understand it. The patient may collapse as they leave the emergency room or even in the toilet while trying to urinate. In all three cases I saw, no urine came out—but later, after death, they wet their pants.

Someone can be talking to you calmly, saying they need to urinate, then stand up alone, and suddenly collapse. I do not understand the physiology behind this. I would like to find out why it happens. I know that one day, in one way or another, I will.

What is fed to the subconscious mind of a patient just before death? Do they somehow signal their body, telling the brain to shut down all systems, bringing a sense of peace, relaxation, and even a strange acceptance of death? We cannot truly say that death brings pleasure. If it did, I do not know how it could be taken willingly. For now, no one wishes for death.

These tragic situations would not happen if hospitals were properly equipped with trained personnel and all the necessary resources to provide safe, quality, and affordable healthcare. If healthcare workers worked in conducive environments, with fair pay and decent living standards, patients would receive proper care. Until that happens, countless cases of patient exploitation will continue in both public and private hospitals, especially affecting those who cannot afford the high costs.

But the government can act. Every citizen deserves safe, quality, and reliable service—not only in healthcare but in all sectors. Deal with corruption and cartels across the board, and we can achieve universal health coverage (UHC) that is safe, good, affordable, and available to everyone.

I cannot stop dreaming that this can happen. Our nation is rich; resources are plenty. We have the power and capacity to achieve this. We only need to be honest with ourselves, feed positive thoughts to our subconscious minds, change our thinking, correct our ways, and do what is right for all. As a country, we can do it.

Let the political class focus on the people—the same people who elect them. Even if improving healthcare is the only thing done right, it would make a tremendous difference. Equip hospitals, stop looting public funds meant for healthcare, and ensure every individual, regardless of socio-economic status, receives quality care.

I have spoken much about healthcare, but does that mean other sectors are better? The education sector, finance, agriculture, tourism, security, sports, water, and foreign affairs—none are without challenges. I speak as a doctor because this is the shoe I wear; other sectors are like shoes worn by others, which I may not fully understand. I trust someone else will address them.

The solution to healthcare challenges is simple: employ enough healthcare workers nationwide, ensure their working environments are safe and supportive, pay them fair wages, and train more staff—then give them jobs. Equip hospitals fully, including basic medicines, so patients do not have to travel long distances for care. Subsidised medicines to make them affordable.

These two steps—trained, well-supported healthcare workers and fully equipped facilities—can transform our health sector. Then, we will be a healthy nation. Healthy people can attend school; learners cannot learn if they are sick. Without a strong education system, we cannot prosper or develop. Make education better for a better nation.

Let us sit together, talk together, reason together, and find ways to eradicate poverty. Give us a break—we are tired of struggling in hardship.

Chapter 15

Our education sector has been deeply affected by the pandemic. The lives of many young girls have been disrupted, and for some, changed forever. The containment measures meant to limit public gatherings and physical contact were not favourable for the youth.

Meanwhile, family get-togethers, house parties, and other social events continued as usual. Ironically, the lockdown provided plenty of time for these gatherings. You cannot imagine what goes on during birthday parties, house parties, or casual meet-ups.

As young people, they must find ways to engage themselves. Even if parents are strict, these events have been happening. We have seen several young girls heavily pregnant, and we do not even know how many have been affected by HIV, AIDS, or other sexually transmitted infections. The growing number of young mothers in our society is proof that much has been happening. Considering economic hardship, if someone could offer even a little money, it was often enough to sway decisions.

A friend of mine shared his experience of lockdown and curfew holidays. He is a seventeen-year-old high-school student. As usual, he would meet his friends in the village, call others to join, and invite friends of the opposite sex. Those who could come, did. During these meetings, he confessed, a lot happened—things so shocking that I cannot even record them in this book.

They could drink any type of alcohol, smoke whatever they could find, and take part in dares, many of which were disgusting. He mentioned watching the girl next door, the adjacent neighbours, as the parents were strict. One or two friends would only need to know about the meeting and its venue for the plans to unfold. Once parents left, the youth would begin their activities.

This continued throughout the curfew and lockdown. When parents were home, the children would behave perfectly, pretending to be good. But behind closed doors, the reality was very different. Very soon, reports of teens caught at house parties, birthday events, and other gatherings engaging in shameful activities became frequent.

Adults often manipulate these teenagers, offering gifts or small amounts of money. Morality seems to have been lost. The government's handling of the pandemic, particularly school closures, left lasting consequences. They now accept that closing schools was a mistake and are allowing even pregnant girls back to school. But what about those who married during this period and will never return to education?

The containment measures caused many businesses to close, with some collapsing completely. Parents struggle to pay school fees, and some do not even know where to send their children because schools have permanently shut down. The government is attempting to reintegrate a few students, especially those in their final years, but some say they are being treated like guinea pigs in an experiment.

I find it difficult to comment fully on the situation. People often ask if the virus is still widespread. One patient even asked: "Why don't doctors and politicians wear masks if the virus is still around? Or is it gone?" I had no clear answer.

Much of the current behaviour of teenagers is rooted in parenting—how they were raised and by whom. A friend shared her own story. She said it wasn't her fault. Her parents left her in the care of nannies while they travelled for work or business for months at a time. Each time they returned, a new nanny would take over. She was too young to understand or report what was happening. She grew up absorbing the behaviours of three different nannies over five critical years, leaving her with lasting unhappiness.

Her experience illustrates how neglect, even by well-meaning parents, can shape the behaviour and choices of young people.

Some people had very bad characters, but others were kind to her. She has a quirky personality, and even her behaviour cannot be traced back to her parents. She does not know whose character she inherited, because she is certain her parents do not possess any of it. Now that she is old enough to protect her siblings, she wants to ensure none of them experience what she endured as a child. She says that as a child, she received no parental love. Her parents left home early in the morning before she woke up and returned in the evening when she was already asleep. This memory still pains her deeply.

She has never shared this experience with anyone—not even her mother. But one thing she is sure of: she will never leave her own children in the hands of strangers. No work or business will ever keep her away from them. The hunger for money that drove her parents shaped her life, but she is determined not to let her children suffer the same way.

Because she is now old enough to distinguish right from wrong, she often has to do strange things just to survive. She avoids sharing her problems with anyone, shaped by what was ingrained in her subconscious as a child. She is extremely secretive, especially about herself, and still feels bitter about what her parents made her endure—even though they are unaware of it.

As a parent, it is vital to examine how you treat your children—both boys and girls. How much freedom do you give them? How much do you take away? If children feel trapped, they will always find ways to survive and do what they are forbidden to do.

Give them the right information. Teach them the realities of life. Do not lock them inside the house or prevent them from seeing their friends. If you try to control everything, they will find secret ways to connect, and you may never know. For example, if you worry about your daughter seeing a boy or bringing someone home without your knowledge, rest assured, they will find a way.

Children are resourceful; they know how to navigate boundaries you set.

You may allow them to attend house parties, go to a cousin's home, or visit places like a play station. Even in these safe environments, children may seize the opportunity to explore what they are not allowed to do elsewhere. These behaviours do not only happen at night; they can happen during the day too. Even swimming pools or family get-togethers, which seem harmless, can become moments where they experience things they usually cannot.

For these reasons, parents often unknowingly contribute to the "weird" or secretive behaviours of their children. A friend once confided that their strict parents never allowed them to leave home, visit friends, or invite anyone over. Naturally, they had to find ways around these restrictions—and they did, just as many other children do today.

Be kind and understanding to your children, and they will share their lives with you. You are not the only parent who is strict, and your children are not the only ones raised under such conditions. What your child does to navigate restrictions, others do as well. Children will find a way whenever an opportunity arises—regardless of where they are, who they are with, or when it happens.

Change the way we think; let us change the way we parent. Let us not focus on money alone. Children are gifts from God—treat them with care and love. I know the money you seek is for their good, to give them a better life than yours. But do not let them suffer in the hands of strangers while you chase wealth or remain absorbed in work. If you lose your job today, someone else will take your place tomorrow. But what happens if you lose your child? Not necessarily to death, but when they grow spoiled, misguided, or distant—who will you blame?

We are quick to blame others for spoiling our children, but the truth is, we are the ones failing them when we neglect proper parenting. Society is suffering because we prioritise work over raising our children well. The better we raise our children, the better our society will become in the future.

Chapter 16

I want to wake up one day and affirm that my immediate neighbour, wherever I may be in our nation, is in complete accord with me. I pray for a spiritual union among us. May divine love flow through our personalities. I know we can give ourselves, as a nation, love, light, peace, and joy.

I believe we can make our lives full, complete, and wonderful. If we all possess four simple qualities among others—spirituality, loyalty, faithfulness, and truth—we will be harmonious, peaceful, and happy. I choose to accept only that which belongs to love, truth, and beauty.

Let us not be scavengers who focus on petty faults or errors in each other. Instead, let us give attention and praise to the constructive and remarkable qualities in others, no matter our differences. Put aside your disagreements, focus on what is constructive, and let us build our nation.

Politics divides us more than anything else. If we could learn to forgive our political opponents, we would become great. We do not have to be enemies because of our political differences. Reflect on your life: how many times has life forgiven you for your mistakes?

Consider this: if you cut yourself by accident, signals are sent to your subconscious intelligence, which immediately sets about repairing the cut. New cells form to close the wound. If you burn your hand, the life principle reduces swelling and congestion, and new skin begins to regenerate. If you eat contaminated food, life forgives by causing you to vomit, preserving you. Life holds no grudges and is always forgiving. It brings you back to health, vitality, harmony, and peace if you cooperate by thinking in harmony with nature.

Let us avoid negative, hurtful memories, bitterness, and ill will. These feelings clutter the mind and block the free flow of life within us.

Speaking to leaders, whether political or otherwise, there is something eating at you inside; otherwise, you would not act as you do. You are punishing yourself, and you must learn to forgive yourself. Do not think that God is punishing you; it is yourself. Do not misuse power, or you will suffer accordingly. Understand that if you hit your hand against the wall, you hurt yourself. When you are in power, use it like electricity. You can choose to use it to light a home or to destroy it.

A politician once quoted the Bible, saying, "Come now, and let us reason together" (Isaiah 1:18). We can reason together and forgive one another. In Mark 11:25, we are told, "And when you stand praying, forgive, if you hold anything against anyone, so that your Father also which is in heaven may forgive you your trespasses." Let us not demonise others. Let us not build ourselves up through negative criticism or constant hatred of those we differ from.

If you train your mind to do something consistently, you will master it. For example, if you drive a car repeatedly, your subconscious automatically takes over, and you drive naturally. In the same way, train your mind to focus on building consensus, not differences.

This message is not only for politicians; it is for all of us. The solutions to our problems lie within the problems themselves. There is an answer to every question you have. If you find yourself in a difficult situation and cannot see the way forward, trust that the infinite intelligence within your mind knows all, sees all, and can do all. It has the answer to every question, the solution to every problem, and the guidance for every action. By trusting this intelligence, a new mental attitude emerges, enabling you to find the right solution and next steps.

If we all cultivate this attitude of mind, we will experience order, peace, understanding, and meaning in all that we do.

Do not live in a prison of your own making in your mind. You are bound only by your beliefs, opinions, training, and the influences of your environment. Your inner fears and instability are affecting your life. Refuse to be a prisoner of yourself. Build freedom, peace, and love in your mind instead of hatred. You simply need to realise that you are capable of doing something good. You would be a fool to continue suffering because of the negative thoughts you have fed into your mind.

Bring change in your mind, bring change in society, bring change in our nation, and bring change to the world.

Your friends' dreams are not greater than yours. The difference lies in what each of us chooses to dream about.

In my own small mind, I have created an environment that is peaceful, filled with wonderful experiences and meaningful achievements. I only had to take one step and act. That simple step was to speak to you, to share my thoughts, and to persuade you to change your mind so that we can be in harmony. So that we can reason together, discuss and agree, and become good neighbours. So that we can fit perfectly into our shared ecosystem.

I feel that the world I have created in my own mind, where I have no enemies, where my neighbours need not know my tribe, where I enjoy freedom, peace, and liberty, is open to all. But do not come to destroy the peace and harmony of this world. Remain in your own.

As I sit in my small office in my hospital, I can visualise a great society that is peaceful and joyful. Children play freely in the courtyards, moving between neighbourhoods without fear. This is the dream I have for our nation, our society, whether it is election time, before elections, or after them.

We do not know what challenges lie ahead. The pandemic has brought new rules.

We are no longer free to do what we have worked for, what we deserve, or what we ought to do.

As a lawmaker and representative of my people, I will not profit from tenders or contracts meant for the public. Instead of taking millions to build roads in my community, I will add two beds to the local health facility, two desks to the primary school in my village, or a small industry for local produce. That is how I can provide the best service to my people. When I retire, I will have peace of mind, knowing I did what I could during my era.

Our media houses, however, continue to give platforms to the senior old guards, experienced in public lies and false conspiracies. Those called for interviews are often the very people who have looted public resources, misused power, and refused to promote peace, choosing instead to divide us.

Those dominating our media do not welcome new ideas. They resist change because if change comes, they risk losing their positions.

We need to call the creative and the thoughtful across all media channels. Invite those with new ideas to speak, those with sober minds to guide us. Those who are famous today have no more ideas. They cling to what made them famous and refuse to change.

There are many brilliant, innovative minds out there capable of building our nation and making it greater.

Do not let those who cling to power speak for us. Do not let those who resist change dominate our conversation on live television. Let them remain in their opinions and ideas. They will continue to suppress us, sell divisive thoughts, and prevent progress. They do not want us to rise out of poverty, because if we do, we will no longer depend on them. They do not want that.

As the media fraternity, bring us change. Bring those with ideas on how to improve our health care to speak to us. Bring those who can make our education system better. Let them appear on TV shows. We do not want old-fashioned thinkers to address us. Let those with ideas to modernise our society speak. Bring them to your programmes. Let those with ideas for building infrastructure across our nation speak to us.

We do not want to see every day those who suppress the rights of teachers, doctors, nurses, farmers, and learners. We do not want to hear from them. We do not want to see them on our screens. We are tired. Give us a break. They will not have a public platform if you do not invite them into your programmes. Cover the stories that matter. Let the media be a channel for change, not a stage for divisive and oppressive politicians. Refuse them public addresses. They will speak only to themselves and sort out their minds privately.

Bring us to TV shows and radio interviews, those who speak to our problems, not their power struggles. Give us meaningful breaking news. Give us positive news about our education system, our health sector, tourism, and agriculture. No news about corruption or looting public funds.

In your programmes, talk about what our hospitals need. Talk about what teachers need to help learners succeed. Talk about what farmers need. Talk about ways to attract foreign investment. Talk about initiatives that bring peace and unity within our borders and with neighbouring countries.

Do not make us believe every day that our nation is run by dynasties and hustlers. Press that button of change as the media. Everything comes to the spotlight through the media, and we can change negative mindsets in our society through it.

If you agree with my idea, act on it. But if you remain rooted in old customs, the daily news will never change. We will remain still like imaginary dams built on air, modern stadiums built in boardrooms but never open to the public, lab projects for a few, while the majority continue learning under trees and at the mercy of nature.

We do not want to be addressed on public holidays with written speeches designed by those entrenched in the system, taught to craft words to suit the occasion, even if it means building homes on trees. Speak to us about what matters to us. Talk about our problems. Tell us how you will handle a pandemic. Tell us what your government is doing to restore sanity to our economy.

Explain why children are not in school. Talk to those who are sick and cannot access local health services. Reassure us that we do not need to live in fear of insecurity. Talk to us about collapsing businesses and rotting farm produce.

Do not tell us to import everything and export nothing. Talk about us first. Sign agreements for our benefit, not yours. Speak on our behalf, not your own.

Talk about the landless. Do not read edited colonial speeches. Speak to us today. If your friend spoke about squatters yesterday, today, tell us how homes have been built for them. Do not dwell on historical injustices. Speak about today, and remember tomorrow is coming.

If you disagreed yesterday, do not tell us to remain stagnant until reconciliation. Resolve your differences privately, but let the country move forward. Do not bring old problems into our newly built forests.

Because of your political differences, our screens have become dull. There is nothing left that draws us to watch them. Your allies now control the media houses. They are presented as the only good news, the only breaking news, day after day. Give us a break.

When the few right-minded country people finally come to power, I ask them to show us the change we have longed for. Deliver the peace and harmony we pledge to have. Do not fall into the same trap of serving only yourselves; do not misuse power. Light our homes. Build schools. Improve our healthcare. Raise our economy to higher levels. Make our agriculture stronger. Improve our businesses and create an environment where they can thrive. Attract investors, but do not sell our country. Do not suffocate us any more than we already are. Do not sink us deeper if we are already barely afloat. Reunite us rather than divide us further.

If you are an employer, make your workers happy. Let them not come to your office or business and lament every day. Be an agent of change.

I believe many great people with fine minds and ideas will read this book. Convince your inner self. Send a signal to your mind, your thoughts, your heart, your bloodstream that enough is enough. Make that move. The decision you have been waiting for can be made now. Just do it. Let us make our environment better. Rebuke that bad habit, that bad behaviour, that poor character, that wrong conspiracy. Do not subscribe to false narratives. Say no.

Read this with spirit. Be in a mood for change. Sink deep into it and say: it is now. It is enough.

Rise up against racism, against nepotism, against favouritism, against hatred, against false accusations and against false pretence. Be who you are. You are not what people think you are. Be yourself. Bring sanity to the system. Bring the change you need.

I long for the day I can speak to the government of the day, speak to the legislature, speak to the elite, and tell them what our society needs is not power, not politics, not hatred, but peace and bread on our tables. I will tell them what it means to encounter poverty. I will speak. I will explain. I will make sure they understand, even if they pretend not to.

Let the last election be the last one to divide us. In the same way, let that poor family, who used to be the laughing stock, be the last such family. Better the lives of people: poverty is killing more than illness does.

Let us not witness public embezzlement on display and then have nothing done about it. Let us see issues dealt with to finality. Facilitate, finance and enable the responsible agencies to tackle corruption, abuse of power and all forms of injustice in good time.

We need not reopen colonial disputes today. We already have enough disputes that need solving right now. We are ready to forgive and move on as a country. We want a better nation; we want to build it. If you will not help us to better our lives and our nation, remain silent in the comfort of your sitting room and watch us move ahead. Nothing will stop us. We are ready to leave behind anyone who stands in our way. Let those warring communities in our nation read this and come to their senses. You have the solutions to your problems; it is only that you do not want to solve them. Peace, love and harmony should be your portion. From now on you will no longer fight with your neighbour because we are united in a common agreement that we should move on as a peaceful community to build and improve our lives. And let the communities already enjoying peace help their neighbours back to peace and harmony.

If I had enough today, I could not sleep until I had made sure everyone had at least something on their table for dinner.

Many of my friends will read this book and say: we saw this, we anticipated this in this young man. But now I urge them all, let us join hands, because this is not a personal roof I am building over my head alone, but a market for all of us. We can do it. We have the potential. We can make our society great. Feed good thoughts about your neighbour and about your politically labelled enemy, and we shall be there. A nation is great when its people have great minds and ideas. Young, vibrant and energetic men ready not to be used against one another, but ready to join hands in nation building. To you belongs power, and to you belongs greatness.

I want, when I go back to my village, for my neighbours' children not to run to see the vehicle I drive, but to share with me the same parking space.

Chapter 17

The unionists are not doing justice. They no longer represent the views of the members but pursue their own self-interest. They meet in lavish hotels, sip tea, and share kilos of roast meat at the expense of those they are meant to serve. They fall into the trap of accepting bribes and cheap offers.

Our union leaders can call for a nationwide strike but retreat at the last moment, simply because someone has offered them trivial favours to call off the industrial action. They enjoy being vocal, appearing in front of cameras, speaking in polished English, rather than confronting the real issues that healthcare workers face, and standing firm against intimidation.

Time and again, industrial action is called, but who suffers in the end? It is the individual healthcare worker. They are suspended, their salaries withheld, and some even lose their jobs.

We need strong leadership in all our unions. People who can fight and push for the rights of healthcare workers.

Imagine a football match. One team goes to the corner of the field to pray and pledge victory. The opposing team copies the act, pretends to pray, and makes louder noises, but at the end of the match, they are defeated. This is what some of our union leaders are doing. They imitate other unions, even when they are unprepared for the actions they advocate. The result is intimidation, weak offers, and premature retreats. This is cowardice.

There are many vibrant union members who raise important issues and offer excellent ideas, but they are too afraid to present them to ministry officials. For these leaders, dining with top officials is considered a major achievement. This is often enough for them to call off industrial actions. Some unions do not even use their own name, hiding behind generic titles that blend them into other healthcare unions. They know they are weak and incapable of creating real change. They fill leadership positions with loyal supporters, leaving those with different views sidelined.

We will be in those top offices. We will restore sanity to the sector. We will clear the mess that has been created. We believe that the pain we feel can drive us to realise our greatest potential.

Why complain about things we have the power to change? When we detach our mind from a situation, its power over us ceases. Let us be courageous. Courage is the strength to let go of the familiar.

Our leaders must stop being cowards. Do not give in to fear. Sometimes fear can make you feel incapable of achieving what will bring happiness. You have the power to talk yourself down, and the power to talk yourself up. Stay wise.

I believe we all have the ability to change almost anything in our lives that we wish to change. Whether we use that power is our choice.

To all leaders, remember that words are powerful. Always use words that encourage, not discourage. Understand that you have power only over your mind, not over outside events. Realise this, and you will find true strength.

Let us remember that in any battle, whether you are a union leader, a political leader, a religious figure, or a CEO, losing is a learning experience. It teaches humility. It teaches you to work harder. It is also a powerful motivator.

Do not be swayed by only what is in front of you. Remember that what lies behind your eyes holds far more power than what you see ahead. Be conscious of your mind. Have your own principles. Do not give anyone the power to insult you simply because they cannot recognise your worth.

When you feel weak, remember how powerful your God has always been in your life.

You often wonder what happens when you elect leaders to represent your needs. They get bribed. Money is the tool used against your demands. Money amplifies human personalities and reveals their true nature.

Many people seek knowledge and then power so they can achieve goals of conquest, control, and manipulation. Insults are the last resort of the weak-minded when they feel powerless.

Approach each morning with the spirit that it is an opportunity to rise with more strength, more determination, and to achieve what you desire. Your decisions hold the only true power you have on earth. Do not give your power away, for anything you allow to control you will do just that.

From observing our leaders, I have learned that fake people worry about maintaining an image, whereas real people simply do not care.

Stop waiting for society to give you permission to be yourself. To remain true to yourself in a world that constantly tries to change you is one of the greatest accomplishments.

Watch those around you—at school, in college, in business, in the office, in the field. I wish people were more like money, so we could lift them and see who is real and who is fake.

Do not allow anyone to turn your voice into an echo, for you were not born to be silenced. Make good friends. Most friendships are like trees: the roots are your real friends, and the fake ones will fall away like leaves. Be real to yourself before you can be real with anyone else. Real people are often hated and unappreciated by fools. I do not need everyone to like me for being nice. I want them to stay because I am real.

Be who you choose to be, not who others expect you to be. If anyone has a problem with you, let them speak to you directly, not through social media. Let them stop talking behind your back. If they have a complaint, let them bring it to your attention. Acknowledge that they heard the rumours, but then show them the real you. I would rather be despised for my character than liked for lacking it.

Sometimes the things we say sarcastically reveal what we truly think deep down.

Poverty is ravaging us all.

At work, I see people trying to impress others with appearances, new clothes, and the latest fashions. Yet at home, landlords close rental houses over overdue arrears and people go to bed hungry. Do not surround yourself with a fake environment. Focus on your attitude, your character, and your morals. Stop worrying about what others will say. True friends praise you behind your back and criticise you to your face. Be your true self. It is better to live imperfectly as yourself than to strive to be what someone else wants.

Time and again, I remind myself that I do not need to hate my haters, but I will never surround myself with negativity because I know I am better than that.

I ask myself many questions, yet some remain unanswered. My inner voice challenges me: would you rather revisit the past or see what the future holds?

Do not let past experiences harm your future. The past cannot be changed, and your future does not deserve punishment.

When I meet friends from well-off families who belittle my achievements, I simply say: Sorry, I was not raised to be sociable like you, but I grew up with unusual experiences and gained remarkable wisdom that makes me see you as foolish. I have my own principles and allow no one to violate them.

Sometimes it takes a painful experience to make us change our ways.

My dad once told me that in everything I do, and wherever I am, I should listen to my elders' advice. Not because they are always right, but because they have more experience of being wrong. That is why I listen.

The presence of my mum and her powerful and kind advice makes me treasure her deeply in my heart. I will always listen to her and love her very much. My prayer to Almighty God is to grant them good health and a long life, to live long enough to see my children and grandchildren.

My mother is a woman of wisdom. She carries herself with humble, quiet grace. Though she did not attend a modern school for a Western education, her presence is powerful and inspiring. Lots of love, Mum. She took us to school to help lift our family out of misery and poverty.

Every time I speak to my mum, I feel inspired. Her inspiration creates a never-ending power that drives me forward. She placed all her hope in God, always prays for us, and always blesses us. Through the strength of her hopes, miracles have happened, and more will happen. Thank you, Mum. Thank you, Dad. Feel loved. God will keep you safe so you can play with your grandchildren as you grow older.

I have chosen to speak to my parents through this book, to remind them of what I once told them. I long to see them play and create stories with our children, as we did with our grandparents. That is my constant prayer to God, to keep them safe until then. I believe that our generous God, full of grace, will grant them good health and life for as long as He wills. I pray this, and I believe God is listening and has already heard. In the mighty name of Jesus Christ, our Saviour. Amen.

When I speak with my parents, I realise the inner strength that is the most powerful tool to help me stand with determination and achieve my goals. They encourage me and keep me in their prayers. My dad once told me, and reminds me often, that I should never stop dreaming. He says that if a man stops dreaming, he is as good as dead.

This advice has given me a positive attitude that puts me in control of my circumstances, rather than letting my circumstances control me. I believe that our thoughts have incredible, life-changing power. I urge you also to make sure that your worst enemy is not living between your own two ears.

I will never give up. I know there is power in perseverance. The world is not changed by the most talented people, but by the most determined. You have more control than you think. There should be no doubt that you have the power to change and control the situation, no matter what it is. Develop courage. Courage is the inner strength that allows you to fight for your very existence and keep trying, even when you know you may fail. Courage and determination make a fighter.

We are trapped in poverty because some of us do not keep trying. Many give up after they fall. Just because you have fallen does not mean you have to stay down. Find a way to get back up. Do not let the fear of failure stop you from trying. Even when you fail, it is not enough reason to give up. There is light at the end. After many trials, you will find success.

Never let the ups and downs along the way stop you from doing what you know is meant for you. Let us not use fear as an excuse for not trying. You may fail, but try anyway. That is how you grow, and that is how you achieve incredible things. Do not be afraid to fight for what is right and for what is better. Understand that it is not important to achieve everything in one go, but it is vital to make positive progress in a reasonable time.

Limits are only a state of mind. You can always push yourself to do better, no matter the cost. Keep going, and you will succeed.

The political elite can tell us that winners often lose far more than losers. So if you keep losing but continue to try, keep going. You are on the right path. Bravo. No matter how many times you fail, you are not a failure until you quit trying. A great victory can follow a shocking defeat if there is persistence and determination in your pursuit. Never say never. Keep your hopes alive. Go for it. Do not quit.

Just because something seems hard to achieve does not mean you should give up. Instead, put in more effort and work harder to reach your goals. You know many people who have failed countless times and still kept going. It is because they have learned that every failure teaches them something valuable.

Some people will always prefer to see you down, but use that as motivation to work harder and grow stronger. Whenever you find yourself doubting how far you can go, remember how far you have already come. Recall everything you have faced, the battles you have won, and the fears you have overcome.

Value yourself, your voice, your body, your opinions, your dreams, your pride, and even your ego. You have a right to take up space. Choose words that are positive and kind, words that empower, encourage, motivate, and help others move towards their goals. Always choose words that heal, not destroy.

For example, in our country, a politician decides to help people in a small but meaningful way. He gives wheelbarrows to youths so they can earn a living. Yet the opposing political elite, instead of supporting this act of kindness, belittle it. They criticise that the tool is old-fashioned. They have been around, too, but what have they actually done? What have they given to the youth? Give us a break!

Stop undermining small but valuable efforts, especially when you cannot do even a fraction of it yourself.

By this, I am not saying you should give us things that will not truly change our lives or improve our economic situation. We want to rise out of poverty. Stop letting us suffer from hunger by infringing on our rights. Build infrastructure for us, provide good quality healthcare, stop corruption, stop stealing public funds, and do not assign government projects and tenders only to your friends and family for personal gain. We do not deserve this. Make our lives better, not miserable. Change the nature of your politics.

As others speak against you, remember that it takes a strong fish to swim against the current. Even a dead fish floats with it.

Our willingness to get our hands dirty has always defined us as a nation. It is a mark of hard work and of joy. Dirt is not our enemy. Our enemies are hatred, bad politics, and corruption. Remove these, and our nation can be beautiful again.

Do not let your victories make you soft. Do not let your defeats make you quit. Do not let your teammates down in any situation.

Chapter 18

Being a doctor is hard work. You work long, exhausting hours. It is emotionally demanding, tense work, and is exposed to every risk of infection. If you do not truly love it, then it is not worth it.

I have also learned that there is only one boss: the customer. They can fire anyone in the company or institution, from top to bottom, simply by taking their business elsewhere.

To my colleagues: offer good, safe, quality service to our clients and patients. Give them your best. Do the right thing. Do not exploit them. They are not responsible for your encounter with poverty.

I have come to understand that it is not because things are difficult that we do not dare and care. It is because we do not dare or care that things become difficult.

A colleague once told me, If you want to go fast, go alone. If you want to go far, go together. We often joked about this during our internship, quoting it whenever we could. Keep pursuing your dreams, my friend. You are a great doctor.

Working in a small private clinic taught me that to perform well, you must be in the trenches. You must do the hard work for many reasons: to build yourself as a performer, to understand your audience, to work diligently, and to wonder, even if you are looked down upon or belittled.

'Do I really want to do this?'

Just remember: if you are willing to do more than you are paid to do, eventually you will be paid to do more than you do.

It is said that all paid jobs absorb and degrade the mind. I now fear that my mind is being absorbed and degraded. What should I do?

I have chosen to think creatively. I must be able to see afresh what I usually take for granted. Do not keep your ideas secret, because in secret they die. They need light and air, or they will starve.

I have worked with people who do not believe what you tell them. They rarely believe what you show them. They often believe what their friends tell them. They always believe what they tell themselves.

But I have learned not to worry about people stealing my ideas. If your ideas are any good, you will have to fight for them.

If you work only for money, you will never succeed. But if you love what you do and always put the customer first, success will come. I have seen friends fail and others succeed. The difference lies in what they worked for. What are you working for?

Sometimes it is good to be selfish. You must claim what you want when you can, before someone else takes it. But that does not mean you only discover your strengths when someone tries to exploit your weaknesses or kindness.

If you do not have what you want right now, it may simply mean it is not meant for you at this time.

I have learned that people we know only briefly can leave a bigger impact on us than those we have known for years.

You only need to appear confident, even when you are not.

I look into the doubting eyes of my patients, who are unsure if they are in the right place or with the right person. Yet I must remain confident. I know I will do the right thing. I believe in myself. I am trained and qualified for this profession. Knowledge and skill are not in my appearance. Sometimes you meet someone who does not look like what you expected, but that does not mean they are unfit for the job. You only need to adjust your attitude to accommodate the change. Respect those who perform their job well, regardless of your initial impression.

In all professions, we start somewhere. We must train, intern, or practice before we are entrusted with power and authority.

You may have been belittled or looked down upon during your internship, but that does not justify doubting interns now. Believe in them, encourage them, teach them, correct them, but do not intimidate or demean them. You may be the CEO today, but tomorrow they may occupy your office. Would you want them to treat your family as you treat them?

Think of the healthcare worker who attended to you in the hospital. It could have been you, a family member, or a friend. That worker was an intern, not yet employed, not on the payroll, not receiving any risk allowance. Yet they worked tirelessly, often without recognition. Someone may have looked down on them or demeaned them. Did they deserve that?

Interns are not destined to remain interns forever. Some will become consultants. What example do you want them to remember? Do good to others as you wish to be treated.

We had different experiences during our internships. Some were challenging, some were memorable. They shaped who we are today.

Chapter 19

Today I was woken by a knock at the door. It was someone from the management office of our apartment. I had not paid the rent for this month. He came to inform me that as soon as I left, he could lock the door with his padlock. I had no choice. He gave me three days to provide a rent receipt and warned that if I failed, he would have no option but to lock me out. He told me there was no reason to live in a house I could not afford and that I should move to a cheaper one, according to my means. He was absolutely right.

But I am a doctor, and I go to work. My wife is a nurse, and she goes to work too. At that moment, she had not yet returned from her night shift.

The previous night, I had been with my brother. My gas ran out while I was cooking. We had to make do with raw Sukuma wiki, though fortunately, I had cooked ugali and fried some eggs.

After leaving the house, I informed my wife that we would be locked out as soon as I left. I requested three more days to pay the rent. But where was I to find the money? I knew very well that I would not have any cash before the end of the month. Both of us are healthcare workers. We are working, yet we cannot afford to pay our bills on time. We earn meagre wages from our workplaces, and we have no alternative sources of income.

Reporting to my workplace at a small children's clinic that morning, I found a couple waiting with their baby at the reception. I walked in, sweating heavily after nearly an hour's journey from home.

As usual, I checked the baby and administered the vaccines due. I was tired, sweating, and confused; my thoughts were tangled with the worry of almost being locked out. The parents were understanding. This was not our first meeting. They asked questions about how their baby was feeding, how long expressed milk could be stored, and whether milk from last month could still be used. I had limited experience with such scenarios, but I had to give accurate information. We spoke at length, far longer than usual that day.

I also explained the vaccination schedule, what to do if a vaccine was missed, and other relevant information. It was a tough morning. These parents usually go to large private hospitals, yet today they were here in our small clinic, looking at me with worry and trust. They were dressed modestly but neatly, and they were understanding. They knew I might not be well-paid, just a young man in my twenties trying to make ends meet.

I know there are many others in situations similar to mine.

That very morning, I received a call from a new number. It was a colleague who was also looking for a job. Two days earlier, I had been contacted by a small clinic where I had left my contact information while job hunting. I had posted in a group from our internship that the clinic needed staff. My number had been given to the lady calling, who assumed I was hiring. She wanted to know if I had found someone, as she was also searching for employment.

In my mind, I wondered how people perceived me. Did they think I was well-off? If only they knew my situation. But these were personal matters, and I could not share them widely. I forwarded the number to the lady so she could contact the caller herself and try her luck.

Earlier, I had applied for a county government job advertised a month ago. I waited with hope, though given our current situation and widespread corruption, I was uncertain whether I would even be shortlisted, let alone offered employment.

That morning, I watched a discussion on television. One participant argued that the current cabinet ministers for health and education are incompetent. Their reasoning was that they had failed the public. Citizens no longer receive adequate healthcare, and we are in the middle of a deadly pandemic. Government health insurance schemes do not cover the disease, forcing individuals to pay from their own pockets, which is leading to many deaths nationwide. The economy is collapsing, and businesses are struggling.

Regarding education, schools are closed. Children are not going to school, and those who were allowed to return, particularly those in their final years, are getting infected. In fact, there has been a reported death of a secondary school student. It is heartbreaking and deeply unfortunate. The Cabinet Secretary, seen publicly insulting education officials, has shown that they were not prepared for the pandemic or for the full reopening of schools. They have failed the nation and should vacate office. But who can we trust to do better? Every one of us has been affected and disoriented by the pandemic.

Health care workers are crying out loudly that they are overwhelmed and understaffed. Meanwhile, we sit unemployed, jobless, our degrees gathering dust. I remember in college, I had to apply for a Higher Education Loans Board (HELB) loan to complete my studies, which I have yet to repay.

During my internship, things worsened. I had to borrow from mobile lending banks. Kenya Commercial Bank (KCB) sends me messages about my loan, which has been in default for almost half a year. M-Swari also demands repayment, sending reminders for months. And now, rent arrears weigh on me. What should I pay first? What can I postpone? I have been negatively listed by the Credit Recovery Company (CRB). They are relentless, demanding repayment. Poverty is real, yet I refuse to be poor. My conscience tells me I am rich, very rich, but my wealth is invisible. When will I encounter real financial abundance as I have with poverty?

Today, I called my brother to explain my situation, knowing he could not help, as he is also unemployed. Still, he assured me that things would be alright. By faith, I knew they would be. I cannot call my parents for help; I had sent them a little cash from my last month's salary to buy food after they had gone hungry for days. My younger brother is at university, and I sent him a small amount for upkeep. Immediate help was simply not available.

It is mid-month, and I am afraid to approach my boss. I do not want them to see my struggle. They think I live comfortably, but that is a lie.

Seated in my consultation room, the environment is quiet, calm, and cool. Outside, I can hear the voices of two or three people talking, distant machinery humming. In my room, the vaccine fridge produces a soft, steady sound. All of this draws me into deep thought about my situation. I am on the verge of eviction. The landlord warned me that if I slept out twice, I would understand the importance of paying rent. But I did not default by choice. Jobs are scarce.

Our political elite promise a million jobs for young people. I wonder what kind of jobs these are, and whether I might be lucky enough to get one. At times, I think I am in the wrong profession. Yet medicine has been my dream since childhood. It is a calling. I do it passionately. I want to be a doctor, nothing else. The joy of helping someone in pain, of hearing a patient say, "Thank you, doctor," is unparalleled.

Yet now, even as a doctor, I face struggles I did not expect. Hopefully, things will change. A colleague faced difficulties, and I could not assist due to my own financial hardship. Another colleague lost a parent, and I could not offer even a shilling of comfort. My closest friend lost a daughter, and again, I could not help. I wonder how they perceive me, but I trust God is in control.

Many of my patients are financially well-off. When they pay their bills, they do so without struggle, often arriving in luxury cars with credit cards in hand. And I, who missed a meal last night, went without breakfast, walked over an hour to work, tired and weary, cannot even hope for a small gesture. A mere two hundred shillings, a cup of tea, would carry me through the month. Yet I cannot beg; I must remain professional. I wonder if anyone else experiences what I do.

Things will change. How far we have come is by God's grace. The story I share here may seem unbelievable to many, even my patients. But as we all seek services from others, I urge you to show respect to the person seated before you in an office, whether they have money or not.

The person you may despise today could be the CEO of the company you work for tomorrow. None of us holds all the power. Be human to everyone, at every level. Offer kindness, even when most people are not kind.

With all these challenges, at the end of the day, if I manage to have a little cash left at the end of the month, I know my parents have nothing, and my brother needs money for his upkeep on campus. I have bills to pay, both current and overdue. Yet, I will still find a way to help someone in need. I may not have enough to clear my own bills, and thinking about saving feels like a dream. But setting that aside, I want the rest of my day to flow smoothly. I believe each problem will resolve itself in time.

Chapter 20

My ambition is to have beautiful encounters, not to make money. The very substance of ambition is merely the shadow of a dream.

I have, for the most part, suppressed my ambitions in order to become who I need to be. I have chosen not to ignore my past, because to do so would jeopardise my future.

Let us not develop bad attitudes. A bad attitude is a disability. Have a healthy attitude; a healthy attitude is contagious. Do not wait to catch it from others — be a carrier.

As a people, without education, we are in a terrible and deadly danger of taking only the educated seriously. If only the government could listen to a few people of goodwill. To restore the people's trust in government, we must reform the way government operates. We are a forward-looking people, and we must have a forward-looking government.

What a foolish attitude we have towards personal stories. We are becoming a nation that accepts nothing and challenges everything.

Do not come and tell us, or try to prove to us, that you are a performer. Your proofs only tell us where to concentrate our doubts about you. You talk too much about building consensus. Build bridges, and then we can build consensus together. Listen to the will of the people. Involve people in government operations. When people become involved in their government, the government becomes more accountable, and our society becomes stronger, more compassionate, and better prepared for the nation's future challenges.

I want to board that plane with a good attitude. I want to catch that plane that flies to a nation free of corruption. I want to board that plane that goes to the United States of our subconscious minds, fed with good thoughts of our neighbours. I want to board that plane to the land of good politics and mature democracy. I want to board that plane to a nation of freedom — freedom of expression, freedom of speech, freedom of life. I want to catch that plane to a nation with a good quality education system. I do not want to miss the flight to a nation with a good health care system. I want to board that plane to a state with sound infrastructure. I do not want to miss that plane heading to a nation with a conducive business environment. I want to board that plane to a state that has beautiful and excellent tourism attractions. I want to board that plane to a nation of people without hatred, people with good morals. I want to board that plane to a nation united by good politics and a good constitution, not divisive politics. I want to be in a nation where the houses of representatives make and pass good laws, not a nation paralysed by division. I chose to travel with that train passing through tunnels and across land from which I cannot be evicted. I do not want to live in a land that has been taken from me in my motherland.

I want to board that plane to a land of equal employment opportunities for all. That plane which goes to a nation where people enjoy their rights — I do not want to miss it. Allow me to board that plane into a nation where I cannot be forced into exile because of my views. I want to call home a nation of abundance, plenty and fertility, peaceful, free and secure. I want to call home a nation free from bloodshed. Home is a nation free of corruption and the looting of public resources. That is the home I want to be proud of.

I strongly believe that this land, this nation, this state can be our beloved country. Join hands with me in these dreams. We can reform our nation. Let us not look back in anger. I believe that the true function of age is memory. Record as fast as you can. I want to find an aim in life before I run out of ammunition. In my middle age, I am frightened, because I know I will grow out of it. None of us is so old that he or she cannot think they might live another year, dream a new dream, or bring the change we want.

Our nation will never be destroyed from outside; we are destroying it ourselves. As a nation, we are limited, not by our abilities, but by our vision. I believe our nation is the home of the brave. So let it be the land of the free. We have real enemies within our nation. These enemies must be found, pursued and defeated. The corrupt!

Chapter 21

The old man lived peaceully with his family. Among his six brothers and two sisters, they all coexisted in harmony. Of them all, the youngest brother seemed the most stubborn. The old man's name was Job. He was the second son in the family. The eldest brother, Tom, was the family head and a respected figure in the village. As a village elder, people admired him for his wisdom and knowledge. He settled disputes among his brothers whenever they arose and served as a role model for all.

The third-born, Samson, was a polite and kind man. Many liked him for his calm and smiling nature. He spoke little, yet carried out his affairs smoothly and quietly. No one dared misbehave with him. He had a short temper that flared quickly, but beneath it, he was a good man.

The fourth brother, Spark, was a humble-looking man with a strong build. He seemed to have some wealth and had been the favourite of their parents. He had started a business young and had never faced real struggles in life. With minimal Western education, he lacked discernment. His wit was shallow, and he often appeared greedy and ill-willed. He was rarely happy when his brothers succeeded. His own family was disorganised, and his children, though educated, were not close to him. Some even rebuked him openly.

The youngest brother, Mike, was honest and kind-hearted. He loved helping people and was well-liked in the family. Full of energy and youth, he made the most of his talents as a renowned footballer. Yet, he had one weakness: women. This weakness had caused tension and even threatened to tear his family apart.

Mike and Spark did not get along, though they lived side by side, separated only by a fence. Their children, however, lived in harmony. Spark accused Mike of influencing his children negatively, while Mike blamed Spark for misfortunes in his own family.

Spark could not be trusted. He spied on his brothers and spoke ill of Mike. Yet Mike paid him no mind. Despite his weakness, Mike caused no conflict in his brothers' households.

Spark was the true enemy. He blamed Mike for every misfortune in his own family and claimed Mike was the source of conflict. But Mike never sought quarrels. Spark was brave, yet reckless. He lied to their brothers before Mike could explain himself, and sadly, they often believed Spark. His actions were driven by selfishness and greed. He never rejoiced in his brothers' successes and worked tirelessly to sow chaos and disorder in their families. Even knowing his nature, the others still trusted him, which remained a mystery.

At one point, Spark had even plotted to harm Job's wife by poisoning her during a ceremony. The plan failed. Job's wife was a kind, wise, selfless woman, full of love and care for everyone. Friends had warned her not to attend, and she avoided the danger.

Both Spark and Tom sometimes harboured ill will toward Job's family, but Job remained steadfast. He prayed for them and believed that any harm they wished upon him would return to their own households. Under God's protection, Job's children thrived. They received a good education and built happy lives for themselves and their families.

Spark and Samson were selfish. They often felt that Job's blessings should belong to them. Samson, though greedy, did not stir conflict. Spark, however, grew restless at the steady progress of Job's family. He tried to create disputes, spreading false suspicions that Mike was pursuing Job's daughters and wife. Job, wise and brave, ignored these lies. His faith in God remained unwavering.

Spark had not succeeded in his schemes. Now, he attempted to turn Job against all his brothers, making him believe that they were a threat to his family. Job, trusting Spark, began to harbour anger against his own siblings. Yet Spark remained the true enemy.

Meanwhile, the next generation overlooked the sibling rivalry. They arranged family gatherings and get-togethers, restoring love and harmony. Though the children had started to go their separate ways, they had yet to confront the real threat to the family. Time would reveal whether Spark could redeem himself. If not, no stone would be left unturned in uncovering his misdeeds.

Spark managed to win Job's daughters to his side, turning them against their father. He even sent some to a sorcerer in an attempt to drive a wedge between Job and his wife. Their aim was to see Job's wife and sons eliminated or forced out. But it is too late for them. All of this has come to the attention of Job's sons. Some of them are seething with anger. Their tempers are burning, and a fight is looming. The rage coursing through their souls spreads like a bush fire. One of them has even sworn that if anything happens to their parents because of the ongoing separation plans, there will be serious consequences. Destiny has been set, waiting for the right moment.

This is the routine in many families across the village.

Chapter 22

For you, Daddy
With a father like you, I feel so blessed.
I feel luckier than all the rest.
You are a guide and you are my friend,
Of all the moments that I spend,
There is always something to learn from you, Dad.
Things of the past and things new
Dad, I just want to confess.
That you are truly the best,
You taught me caring,
I love you, Dad, so strong,
Your meaning in my life, Dad, is so very pure.
The lessons that you have taught me, Dad, I will forever follow.
The meaning of everything, thanks, Dad,
You were strict at times, now good morals I have,
Being lenient at the prime
Dad, you are the best in everything you do,
I just want to tell you
That you mean a lot, and I say it from my heart, Daddy.
You told me never to stop dreaming, Dad.
You raised us with a lot of wisdom,
Every time you are in my prayers and thoughts.
May God grant you good health and many days to see my children and grandchildren!
I love you so very much, Dad.
You gave us everything, by your mere presence,
Fragile in your heart, yet you are strong,

Courageously, you defend your children even when they are wrong,
You taught us how to make the right decisions,
And how to believe in ourselves and our ambitions.
I wish to thank you, Dad, with all my heart today,
You give me advice when I am doing wrong,
You motivate me when I need to be strong.
I love you so very dearly, Dad.

Chapter 23

For you, Mummy,
For nine months, you held me safe in your womb,
You nurtured me till I learnt how to eat with a spoon.
You held my tiny hand and taught me how to walk,
One word after another, you taught me how to talk,
All that I am, I owe to you, dearest mother,
You are so special to me, like no other.
Sweet and compassionate, loving and tender,
A beautiful lady with an even more beautiful heart,
Without you, my whole world will fall apart, mother,
Your love, dear mommy, goes beyond everything else,
You shaped up my life and made up for the mess.
Mom, you are no less than an angel to me,
I have placed your picture within my heart, mother.
There cannot be a better gift to me than you, mother.
Your heart is so clean, beautiful, and strong, yet so very kind and mild.
Your loving mother is so unique and so very rare,
No matter how much time passes, your love will just never wear off in me.
You have washed away my painful wounds and my heart within my mother.
You stayed with me in the hospital the whole time when I was young and got sick,
You have showered me with so much love and care, mother,
You taught me how to dress up, even combing my hair, mother,
You loved me unconditionally, even when I hurt you, Mother.

I will never be able to thank you enough for all that you have done for me,
My love for you, mother, goes deeper than even the deepest sea.
Mom, you are the most beautiful soul on earth,
You are the reason why I smile,
You are the reason why I am happy all the while,
You are the reason why I give my best as a doctor,
You are my inspiration for everything,
You are my world, you mean a lot to me, Mother.
You are in my prayers and thoughts,
In my life, you have the most important role, mother.
I love you, Mom.
Mom, so many things that I have learned from you,
You taught me how to care,
You taught me that I should share,
You taught me to smile in pain,
You taught me to try again,
You taught me the good and bad,
You cheered me when I was sad,
I want to tell you, Mother, I love you to the core.

Chapter 24

Some of my dreams are big, while others are small and simple. No matter their size, they bring me peace. Even when I can't do certain things, my dreams carry me to a new world. They make me smile, even if just for a moment. Dreams really are a blessing.

Today, while others celebrate freedom, I sit alone by my window in a small rented room. Poverty keeps me inside, making me hesitant to go out and connect with others. I long for freedom too—a day when I have money in my pocket and a voice in the world. For now, I have to wait before I can truly call myself free, living in a place where everything I own fits in one small room. Sometimes I wish someone could help carry my burdens, but I hold on to the hope that these hard times will pass. I believe happiness and peace will come and stay. Life can go wrong and feel overwhelming, and I often feel lost. Still, I try to be gentle with myself and keep believing that things will get better.Last night, I dreamed of rivers, streams, animals on the ground, and birds soaring above. I imagined a country where no one knew hate, where people didn't blame their fate, and where hearts were full of love. In my dream, adults were innocent and kind, and no child ever went to bed hungry. People shared what they had, and forgiveness and compassion brought everyone together like a family. There was no division from politics, no leaders stealing from the public, and jobs were given based on merit. People supported their government because it served them well. When I woke up, I realised my dream was far from reality. Still, I promised myself to work toward making it come true. I want to build real connections, not use others for personal gain. I hope for a nation where we listen to each other, find common ground, and live in peace.

Tonight, I had another dream. I imagined visiting peaceful places where I could speak freely and feel a special kind of comfort. These secret dreams always make me smile and lift my spirits. The dreams I cherish most are the ones that come from deep inside me.

Dreaming is just a fantasy!

When I think about tomorrow, I fill my mind with hopeful thoughts. What I want most is a special kind of peace. I don't want to give up, because my dreams are my friends and they feel real to me. In my dreams, life looks just the way I wish it could be. I'm working toward that life, step by step.

I never judge my dreams or let them fade away. I want my dreams to speak for me. There aren't many things I wish for, but I give my best effort because life can always change. My dream might come true.

I dream of a life filled with wonder, where I find peace and kindness from others. I hope to have what I want and to live freely, without stress or struggle. I wish for my dream to become real one day.

Dreams feel so real and wonderful, but when I wake up, they disappear. I wish I could hold on to them longer and finish the happy story they bring. I hope I can have the same dream again tonight.

Some dreams feel close enough to touch. In them, the world is beautiful and everything seems possible. It's a time when I can truly be myself, feel lifted up, and see life in bright colours.

I know my dreams might not come true, but I still hold on to hope. They help ease my pain, even if just for a moment. In my dreams, I can do what I want and find comfort, even if only for a night.

Tonight, it's just me and my dreams. I believe it's important to hold on to your dreams and look forward, because they can help you get through tough times. Dreams give hope for a better life and remind us that things can change.

Dream big tonight, and let your dreams bring you joy.

My dreams mean a lot to me. They take me to a world of imagination, where I can truly be myself and nothing feels fake. My dreams show who I am and what I hope for. I hold on to them carefully, as if they were fragile. Without my dreams, life would feel empty. In my dreams, I feel free, floating in the sky. I long for a place to call home, maybe by a river or in the hills. My dreams fill me with energy and excitement.

We dream of many things as children, but do we have the strength to make them real and live the way we want? As we grow up and face life's challenges, we often let go of our dreams, and that's when we truly lose.

9 789347 397967

Printed at Repro India Ltd.